Contents

List of resources   3
Introduction   4
How to use the CD-ROM   5

Interdependence and adaptation   PAGE 7
Notes on the CD-ROM resources   8
Notes on the photocopiable pages   14
Photocopiable pages   15

Micro-organisms   PAGE 22
Notes on the CD-ROM resources   23
Notes on the photocopiable pages   27
Photocopiable pages   29

More about... dissolving/ reversible and irreversible changes   PAGE 35
Notes on the CD-ROM resources   36
Notes on the photocopiable pages   41
Photocopiable pages   42

Forces in action   PAGE 48
Notes on the CD-ROM resources   49
Notes on the photocopiable pages   52
Photocopiable pages   53

How we see things   PAGE 55
Notes on the CD-ROM resources   56
Notes on the photocopiable pages   58
Photocopiable pages   60

Changing circuits   PAGE 68
Notes on the CD-ROM resources   69
Notes on the photocopiable pages   72
Photocopiable pages   74

GU00900 26

IF YOU ACCEPT THE ABOVE CONDITIONS YOU MAY PROCEED TO USE THIS CD-ROM

30108   022926450

Text © Carole Creary and Gay Wilson
© 2004 Scholastic Ltd

Published by Scholastic Ltd, Villiers House,
Clarendon Avenue, Leamington Spa,
Warwickshire CV32 5PR

Printed by Bell & Bain Ltd, Glasgow
1 2 3 4 5 6 7 8 9 0   4 5 6 7 8 9 0 1 2 3

British Library Cataloguing-in-Publication Data
A catalogue record for this book is available from
the British Library.

ISBN 0-439-98497-1

**Visit our website at
www.scholastic.co.uk**

CD developed in association with
Footmark Media Ltd

Authors
Carole Creary and Gay Wilson

Editor
Christine Harvey

Assistant Editor
Jane Gartside

Series Designer
Joy Monkhouse

Designer
Catherine Mason

Cover photographs
© Photodisc,
Digital Vision

Acknowledgements

Extracts from the National Curriculum for England © Crown copyright material is reproduced with the permission of the Controller of HMSO and the Queen's Printer for Scotland.

Every effort has been made to trace copyright holders and the publishers apologise for any omissions.

List of Resources on the CD-ROM

The page numbers refer to the teacher's notes provided in this book.

Interdependence and adaptation

Carrots, Dandelion, Pot Plant, Tree, Blown down tree	8
Healthy house plant, Healthy geranium, Geranium deprived of light, Plant deprived of water	9
Otter, Shrew, Mouse, Fox, Vetch, Rose bay willow herb, Teasel, Buddleia	10
Caterpillar eating leaf, Bird eating berries, Bee on a flower, Squirrel eating acorns, Lions in shade of tree, Cowpat	10
Rose bush, Greenfly, Ladybird, Grass, Sheep, Human child, Cabbage, Cabbage white caterpillar, Robin, Hawk	11
Wading birds, Seaweed in sea, Bluebells in wood	12
Seashore, River, Woodland	13

Micro-organisms

Child with measles, Mouth showing cavities, Child cleaning teeth, Child washing hands	23
Video: Interview with GP	24
Mouldy apple, Mouldy bread	25
Yeast, E-coli	25
Separating curds and whey, Preparing the curd, Blue cheese	26
Edward Jenner, Louis Pasteur, Lady Mary Wortley-Montagu	27

More about... dissolving/reversible and irreversible changes

Sewage plant	36
Video: Water evaporating from a muddy footprint	37
Cake mixture in basin, Baked cake, Raw egg, Fried eggs, Uncooked bread dough, Baked loaves, Chocolate, Melted chocolate, Ice block, Melting ice cubes	38
Hazard label (furniture), Hazard label (correction fluid)	39
Gas hob with pan, Coal fire, Log fire, Barbeque, Fireworks, Video: paper burning	40

Forces in action

Astronaut on Moon, Astronauts in space, Weightlessness in spacecraft, Mug on elastic band, Paperclip on bar magnet, Divers, Bungy jumper, Parachutist	49

How we see things

Mirror showing back of head, Side mirror on car, Hall of Mirrors at funfair, Dentist's mirror	56
Woman reflected in mirror, Shadow on wall	57

Changing circuits

No entry sign, Turn left sign, Humpback bridge sign, Speed camera sign, Electrical component symbols	69
Circuit diagram: Alternating flasher	70
Fuse box, Overloaded electrical socket	70
Engineer working on a computer server	71

INTRODUCTION

This book and CD-ROM support the teaching and learning set out in the QCA Scheme of Work for science in Year 6. The CD provides a large bank of visual and aural resources. The book provides teacher's notes, which offer background information, ideas for discussion and activities to accompany each of the CD resources. Photocopiable pages are included on the CD and in the book to support the teaching. All the resources have been specifically chosen to meet the requirements for resources listed in the seven QCA units for Y6, although units 6C and 6D have been amalgamated here. Some additional resources and ideas have also been included to enable teachers to develop and broaden these areas of study if they wish. These include such things as stories, information sheets and sheets to help children clarify their thinking or record things they find out.

The resources and activities do not provide a structure for teaching in themselves, but are designed to provide a basis for discussion and activities which focus on the knowledge, skills and understanding required by the National Curriculum for science. Some of the ideas build on the National Curriculum requirements and help to broaden the children's experiences.

In the activities suggested in the book the children are encouraged to develop such skills as observing, questioning, describing, sorting, sequencing, finding out, speaking, listening, reading, writing and drawing. They are increasingly encouraged to devise their own fair tests and to record their findings in a variety of ways.

Links with other subjects
Literacy
There are a number of close links between the topics covered in this book and work on literacy. The discussion activities contribute directly to the requirements for speaking and listening. Opportunities for children to research and debate some of the issues raised in the units enable them to hone and increase their skills. Some of the stories and information sheets could be used as a basis for developing comprehension skills during the Literacy Hour, or to provide a stimulus for shared, guided or independent writing. There is considerable opportunity for children to develop their independent writing skills as they produce leaflets, diaries or write poems using the word cards. Pictures from the CD can be printed to stimulate independent writing or to illustrate it.

Maths
Skills such as counting, matching, ordering or sequencing are essential to both science and maths. Sorting skills are required when using keys to identify and classify organisms. Children are expected to become more accurate in their measuring skills and to use a wider range of measuring instruments.

History
Children find out about famous scientists from the past, such as Jenner and Pasteur and their work with micro organisms. In their work on electricity the children find out about Michael Faraday and how he realised the potential of electrical energy. They are encouraged to further their knowledge by carrying out their own research into these, and other, scientists.

Art and design
The activities in the 'How we see things' chapter, encourage children to explore and use different media to produce the desired effect in making self-portraits from a reflective surface. They can also make shadow puppets, from templates provided, to investigate further and consolidate their understanding of how shadows are formed.

ICT
Children are encouraged to use the Internet whenever possible to search for more information on subjects that they are studying.

HOW TO USE THE CD-ROM

Windows NT users
If you use Windows NT you may see the following error message: 'The procedure entry point Process32First could not be located in the dynamic link library KERNEL32.dll'. Click on **OK** and the CD will autorun with no further problems.

Setting up your computer for optimal use
On opening, the CD will alert you if changes are needed in order to operate the CD at its optimal use. There are three changes you may be advised to make:

Viewing resources at their maximum screen size
To see images at their maximum screen size, your screen display needs to be set to 800 x 600 pixels. In order to adjust your screen size you will need to **Quit** the program.

If using a PC, open the **Control Panel**. Select **Display** and then **Settings**. Adjust the **Desktop Area** to 800 x 600 pixels. Click on **OK** and then restart the program.

If using a Mac, from the **Apple** menu select **Control Panels** and then **Monitors** to adjust the screen size.

Adobe Acrobat Reader
To print high-quality versions of images and to view and print the photocopiable pages on the CD you need **Adobe Acrobat Reader** installed on your computer. If you do not have it installed already, a version is provided on the CD. To install this version **Quit** the 'Ready Resources' program.

If using a PC, right-click on the **Start** menu on your desktop and choose **Explore**. Click on the **+** sign to the left of the CD drive entitled 'Ready Resources' and open the folder called 'Acrobat Reader Installer'. Run the program contained in this folder to install **Adobe Acrobat Reader**.

If using a Mac, double click on the 'Ready Resources' icon on the desktop and on the 'Acrobat Reader Installer' folder. Run the program contained in this folder to install **Adobe Acrobat Reader**.

PLEASE NOTE: If you do not have **Adobe Acrobat Reader** installed, you will not be able to print high-quality versions of images, or to view or print photocopiable pages (although these are provided in the accompanying book and can be photocopied).

QuickTime
In order to view the videos and listen to the audio on this CD you will need to have **QuickTime version 5 or later** installed on your computer. If you do not have it installed already, or have an older version of **QuickTime**, the latest version is provided on the CD. If you choose to install this version, **Quit** the 'Ready Resources' program.

If using a PC, right-click on the **Start** menu on your desktop and choose **Explore**. Click on the **+** sign to the left of the CD drive that is entitled 'Ready Resources' and open the folder called 'QuickTime Installer'. Run the program contained in this folder to install **QuickTime**.

If using a Mac, double click on the 'Ready Resources' CD icon on the desktop and then on the 'Acrobat Reader Installer' folder. Run the program contained in this folder to install **QuickTime**.

PLEASE NOTE: If you do not have **QuickTime** installed you will be unable to view the films.

Menu screen
▶ Click on the **Resource Gallery** of your choice to view the resources available under that topic.
▶ Click on **Complete Resource Gallery** to view all the resources available on the CD.
▶ Click on **Photocopiable Resources (PDF format)** to view a list of the photocopiables provided in the book that accompanies this CD.
▶ **Back**: click to return to the **opening screen**. Click **Continue** to move to the **Menu screen**.
▶ **Quit**: click **Quit** to close the menu program and progress to the **Quit screen.** If you quit from the **Quit screen** you will exit the CD. If you do not quit you will return to the **Menu screen**.

Resource Galleries
▶ **Help**: click **Help** to find support on accessing and using images.
▶ **Back to menu:** click here to return to the **Menu screen**.
▶ **Quit:** click here to move to the **Quit screen** – see **Quit** above.

Viewing images

Small versions of each image are shown in the Resource Gallery. Click and drag the slider on the slide bar to scroll through the images in the Resource Gallery, or click on the arrows to move the images frame by frame. Roll the pointer over an image to see the caption.

▶ Click on an image to view the screen-sized version of it.

▶ To return to the Resource Gallery click on **Back to Resource Gallery**.

Viewing videos

Click on the video icon of your choice in the Resource Gallery. In order to view the videos on this CD, you will need to have **QuickTime** installed on your computer (see 'Setting up your computer for optimal use' above).

Once at the video screen, use the buttons on the bottom of the video screen to operate the video. The slide bar can be used for a fast forward and rewind. To return to the Resource Gallery click on **Back to Resource Gallery**.

Listening to sound recordings

Click on the required sound icon. Use the buttons or the slide bar to hear the sound. A transcript will be displayed on the viewing screen where appropriate. To return to the Resource Gallery, click on **Back to Resource Gallery**.

Printing

Click on the image to view it (see 'Viewing images' above). There are two print options:

Print using Acrobat enables you to print a high-quality version of an image. Choosing this option means that the image will open as a read-only page in **Adobe Acrobat** and in order to access these files you will need to have already installed **Adobe Acrobat Reader** on your computer (see 'Setting up your computer for optimal use' above). To print the selected resource, select **File** and then **Print**. Once you have printed the resource **minimise** or **close** the Adobe screen using — or **X** in the top right-hand corner of the screen. Return to the Resource Gallery by clicking on **Back to Resource Gallery**.

Simple print enables you to print a lower quality version of the image without the need to use **Adobe Acrobat Reader**. Select the image and click on the **Simple print** option. After printing, click on **Back to Resource Gallery**.

Slideshow presentation

If you would like to present a number of resources without having to return to the Resource Gallery and select a new image each time, you can compile a slideshow. Click on the **+** tabs at the top of each image in the Resource Gallery you would like to include in your presentation (pictures, sound and video can be included). It is important that you click on the images in the order in which you would like to view them (a number will appear on each tab to confirm the order). If you would like to change the order, click on **Clear slideshow** and begin again. Once you have selected your images – up to a maximum of 20 – click on **Play slideshow** and you will be presented with the first of your selected resources. To move to the next selection in your slideshow click on **Next slide**, to see a previous resource click on **Previous slide**. You can end your slideshow presentation at any time by clicking on **Resource Gallery**. Your slideshow selection will remain selected until you **Clear slideshow** or return to the **Menu screen**.

Viewing on an interactive whiteboard or data projector

Resources can be viewed directly from the CD. To make viewing easier for a whole class, use a large monitor, data projector or interactive whiteboard. For group, paired or individual work, the resources can be viewed from the computer screen.

Photocopiable resources (PDF format)

To view or print a photocopiable resource page, click on the required title in the list and the page will open as a read-only page in **Adobe Acrobat**. In order to access these files you will need to have already installed **Adobe Acrobat Reader** on your computer (see 'Setting up your computer for optimal use' above). To print the selected resource select **File** and then **Print**. Once you have printed the resource **minimise** or **close** the Adobe screen using — or **X** in the top right-hand corner of the screen. This will take you back to the list of PDF files. To return to the **Menu screen**, click on **Back**.

INTERDEPENDENCE AND ADAPTATION

Content and skills

This chapter links to Unit 6A 'Interdependence and adaptation' of the QCA Scheme of Work for science at Key Stage 2. The Interdependence and Adaptation Resource Gallery on the CD-ROM, together with the teacher's notes and photocopiable pages in this chapter, can be used in the teaching of this unit.

As with the QCA Scheme of Work, this chapter helps children to extend their understanding of plants and animals in their habitats. They revisit work on food chains and consider the interdependence of all living things. They look particularly at the role of green plants and their nutritional requirements.

The teacher's notes suggest ways of using the resources on the CD as a whole class, for group work or with individual children. Some of the activities suggested will link with other areas of the curriculum, such as English, maths, history or ICT. Wherever possible the activities encourage children to ask questions and develop an enquiring approach to their learning.

Resources on the CD-ROM

The resources in this Resource Gallery include photographs of healthy plants, a plant that has been kept in the dark and one kept without water in order to demonstrate some of the requirements for healthy growth. Pictures of carrots, a dandelion root, the roots of a pot plant and tree roots illustrate different root systems and how extensive some may be.

A series of photographs of plants and animals can be used by the children when making and using simple keys. Other photographs show relationships between plants and animals, eg a caterpillar eating a leaf and a bee on a flower collecting and delivering pollen. Photographs of wading birds on a lake and bluebells in a wood, illustrate animals and plants in their habitats.

There are also a series of photographs of organisms, for example a rose bush, an aphid and a ladybird, that the children can sort and order to make food chains.

Photocopiable pages

The photocopiable pages in the book are also provided in PDF format on the CD-ROM and can be printed out from there. They include:
▶ word and sentence cards containing essential vocabulary and phrases
▶ step-by-step instructional sheets
▶ a template for creating an identification key
▶ a puzzle sheet.

Science skills

Skills such as observing, questioning, researching, sorting, sequencing, listening, speaking, reading and writing are involved in the activities suggested in this chapter. For example, finding out about and debating the issues concerning genetically modified (GM) crops will encourage research skills and give an opportunity to practise speaking and listening skills. Devising questions to make a key encourages children to think logically and sort things according to observable features.

NOTES ON THE CD-ROM RESOURCES

ROOTS

Carrots, Dandelion, Pot plant, Tree, Blown down tree

Different types of plants have different root systems, but all roots serve to take up water and nutrients to help a plant to grow, as well as helping to anchor the plant firmly in the ground. Some plants, such as dandelions and carrots, have strong taproots, while others have fibrous, spreading roots, like the tree. The root system of a tree will often spread as widely underground as the canopy spreads above ground, as the photograph and illustration here show. Some plants, like carrots, store food in their roots.

Because a pot plant is in a limited environment it is important to provide extra nutrients to maintain the plant in good health. Its roots will continue to grow until they fill the pot, at which point the plant will need repotting into a larger pot in order to continue growing.

Discussing the pictures

▶ Look at the pictures with the children and discuss the differences between the root systems of the plants.

▶ Ask the children to tell you what they remember about the function of the roots of a plant. Talk about how they absorb water and nutrients, and how they anchor the plant in the ground.

▶ Look at the photograph 'Blown down tree'. Ask the children to look carefully at the roots that can be seen in the uprooted tree and what they notice about them. Point out how the roots are as long as some of the branches. Show the children the 'Tree' illustration and discuss how the roots are as wide as the tree's canopy. Explain that a tree is a very large plant – some are the biggest living organisms and can weigh several tons. Tell them how trees need a strong root system to anchor them in the ground, and also to collect sufficient water and nutrients to sustain them.

▶ Ask the children if they think plants need soil to grow. Tell the children that many commercial crops are grown hydroponically. No soil or compost is used; instead plants are grown in water enriched with the necessary nutrients. Discuss the advantages of this method for the growers – plants do not get dirty and are easier to harvest, saving time and money.

▶ Tell the children how nutrients are sometimes added to the soil or compost in which plants are grown in order to help them make their food using sunlight. If the soil or compost has grown several crops, or a plant has been in a pot for some time, the nutrients may be depleted and need renewing.

Activities

▶ As a class, grow an onion or hyacinth bulb balanced on the top of a jar of water. Ask the children to keep a diary of the root growth. Do the roots appear before or after the first shoot?

▶ Take the class outside to find a dandelion and dig it up with as much root remaining as possible. Cut the root into short lengths, about 2 centimetres long. Let groups of children plant each in a small pot of compost and await the results, recording what happens.

▶ Investigate if all roots behave in the same way as dandelion roots. Let the children try growing carrots, parsnips, daisies or other plants from root cuttings and observe whether a new plant grows or not. (Not all plants can be propagated in this way.) The children could compile a list of those that do grow new plants and those that don't.

▶ Devise a fair test to investigate the effects of using fertiliser when growing crops. Water pots of seedlings or pot plants with varying amounts of nutrients to find the optimum dose.

▶ Give the children a copy of 'Make your own liquid fertiliser' (photocopiable page 18).

PLANT NEEDS

Healthy house plant, Healthy geranium, Geranium deprived of light, Plant deprived of water

Plants need light, warmth and water to grow healthily. Children often think that soil is also essential, but as long as plants receive sufficient nutrients, for example when grown

hydroponically, soil is not necessary. The level of light, warmth and water required varies according to the species of the plant and the habitat in which plants grow. Plants deprived of any of these essentials, however, will become unhealthy and will eventually die. The plants in these photographs show two healthy plants, and the same plants three weeks later after they have been deprived of water and light respectively. The children will be able to see clearly the effects of taking away one of the essential elements that plants need to grow and be healthy.

Make sure that the children understand the difference between nutrients taken up by plants and 'food'. We often talk about 'feeding' plants when in fact plants make food for themselves and other creatures. In reality we supply nutrients to plants which enable them to photosynthesise more efficiently and thus make more plant material (biomass). Children do not need to understand the process of photosynthesis at this stage, but it is helpful to talk about the fact that plants are able to make their own food using the energy of the Sun.

Discussing the photographs

▶ Ask the children to compare the photographs and to identify which two look unhealthy.

▶ Can the children suggest why these plants might be unhealthy? Discuss how a plant needs light, warmth and water to maintain healthy growth.

▶ Ask if all plants need exactly the same conditions to grow. Talk about how some plants are sun lovers and thrive in full sunlight, while others prefer the shade. Discuss organisms such as fungi or parasitic plants, such as mistletoe, which take nutrients from other plants or decaying material.

▶ Talk about carnivorous plants that grow in very poor soil conditions and supplement their needs by digesting small insects. For example, Sundew has very sticky leaves to trap small insects, while the Venus Fly Trap has specially adapted leaves with a mechanism that catches insects by snapping shut when an insect alights on them.

▶ Discuss the fact that plants produce material for new growth for themselves from air and water in the presence of light. Talk about plants being able to make their own material (biomass) in order to grow. Talk about animals needing to take in food in order to grow and repair themselves but plants can make new tissue themselves using water, air (carbon dioxide) and sunlight.

Activities

▶ Give the children the 'Plant growth sentence cards' on photocopiable page 16. Print the photographs of the four plants from the Resource Gallery and ask the children to label them with the sentence cards.

▶ Carry out a class experiment using three similar plants. Place one in a well-lit place (not direct sunlight) and ask a group of children to care for it by watering it regularly. Place another plant in a black bag or box. Ask a group of children to keep it watered but to exclude light from its growing conditions. Place the third plant in a well-lit place but do not water it. Get the class to observe what has happened to each of the plants after two or three weeks.

▶ Investigate the requirements for healthy plant growth by letting the children grow cress under different conditions in film canisters. Show them how to place a good teaspoonful of compost in several film canisters and how to plant one or two cress seeds in each. They can then experiment with plant needs by leaving the lid off one or two canisters, placing the lid firmly on others, watering some with tap water and others also with a plant nutrient. Ask the children to devise a fair test for this investigation.

▶ Mark out three areas (each about 1 metre square) on the school field or other convenient area of grass, in order for the children to see how grass grows under different conditions. (Ensure that the area is safe and doesn't have any faeces or broken glass on it.) Cover one area with black plastic, apply plant nutrient to the second and leave the third as a control. Compare the results after about a week and get the children to take photographs to record the results. (The grass covered by black plastic will begin to go yellow and die, showing that plants need light to grow. The grass watered with nutrients should grow greener and more lush than the control. Let the children use the 'Plants need…' sheet (photocopiable page 19) to record their results.

▶ As a class activity, grow some healthy plants from seeds or cuttings in advance of the school fête or similar event.

KEYS

Otter, Shrew, Mouse, Fox, Vetch, Rose bay willow herb, Teasel, Buddleia

Keys are a useful tool in helping children to identify and classify living things. They are particularly useful when a new species is found. Children need to understand that questions for a key have to be very specific and can only have a 'yes' or 'no' answer.

These photographs show a variety of plants and animals. Some of the photographs can be easily separated in order to make a key using observable features, like the otter and the teasel. Some of the photographs feature organisms where the differences are less apparent, for example the mouse and the shrew.

Discussing the photographs
▶ Remind the children of the work they did in Year 4 about keys.
▶ Ask the children why keys are useful. Talk about how they help us to classify and identify unknown plants or animals.
▶ Talk about how keys can become increasingly complex, using very small differences to distinguish one organism from another.
▶ Look at the photographs with the children and discuss how they could easily be divided into two groups. Remind the children that each question can only have a 'yes' or 'no' answer when using a key.

Activities
▶ Give each child a copy of the photographs and ask them to devise their own key that would identify each of the organisms. (Children may come up with different ways of separating the organisms by asking different questions.)
▶ In pairs, ask each child to pass their key to their partner to use. Can they identify each organism? The children could also visit Year 4 or Year 5 classes to see if the children can use their keys.
▶ Make a collection of inanimate objects and ask the children to devise a key to identify them. This will focus the children on the difficult task of devising 'yes'/'no' questions.
▶ Ask the children to draw some fictitious creatures or plants and to make a key in order for their friends to identify them.
▶ Take the children out and collect minibeasts from the locality. Let the children devise keys to identify them. They could also use keys on the Internet to identify the minibeasts. Show them how to use a search engine to find such keys (supervise their selections to ensure that the websites they choose are suitable, or find some before the lesson and save them in your 'favourites' folder for the children to use).

INTERDEPENDENCE

Caterpillar eating leaf, Bird eating berries, Bee on a flower, Squirrel eating acorns, Lions in shade of tree, Cowpat

Children need to understand that plants and animals are dependent upon each other. For example, birds that use trees for shelter and nesting often eat the fruits from that tree and then disperse the seeds. Bees and other insects visiting flowers to collect nectar carry pollen from flower to flower, thus helping to pollinate them. All species, except plants, depend on each other for food.

These photographs show a range of different dependencies between plants and animals. The photographs of the caterpillar, bird, squirrel and bee show how animals feed on plants. The photograph of the lions demonstrates how an animal can rely on a plant for needs other than food. The cowpat is an example of how animal droppings can provide food for other animals. Notice the flies feasting! The cowpat also helps to fertilise the soil, thus helping plant growth by returning nutrients to the earth as it rots.

Discussing the photographs
▶ Ask the children to tell you what they remember about food chains and other ways in which plants and animals might need each other.
▶ Show the children the photograph 'Caterpillar eating leaf' and talk about how plants

provide food for many animals. Ask the children if they can think of other examples and show them the photograph 'Bird eating berries' or 'Squirrel eating acorns'

▶ Look at the photograph 'Lions in shade of tree' and talk about how animals take advantage of plants in other ways, for example nesting in trees and hedges.

▶ Discuss how animals help plants by aiding seed dispersal. Look at the photograph 'Bee on a flower' and discuss how the bee is pollinating the flowers. Discuss other ways in which animals help with seed dispersal. For example, sheep with burdock burrs on their coats.

▶ Look at the 'Cowpat' photograph and discuss how animals also help to fertilise the land with their droppings. For example, cows and sheep in fields, hippopotami in rivers.

▶ Talk about how sometimes animals depend on other animals. For example, ants, who farm aphids for their honeydew, or the small birds that feed by providing a tooth cleaning service for crocodiles.

▶ Explain to the children how a parasite, such as mistletoe, relies on getting nutrients from other plants, such as apple trees, but does not give anything back to the tree in return. Fungi are not plants, but perform a service in breaking down plant and animal tissue and returning the nutrients to the earth.

Activities

▶ Ask the children to make two lists: ways in which a plant might benefit from association with an animal, and ways in which an animal might benefit from a plant.

▶ In groups, ask the children to research and prepare a short presentation about how animals help plants to disperse their seeds.

▶ Take the children outside and look for evidence of interdependence between plants and animals. For example, look for signs that leaves have been eaten by a small creature, or look under leaves for any insect eggs. Are there any nests or webs? Ask the children what benefits the plant might receive in general. For example, pollination.

▶ As a class, make a list of living things that are parasitic rather than interdependent. Let groups of children use the Internet to find out more and to write about a parasite.

FOOD CHAINS

Rose bush, Greenfly, Ladybird, Grass, Sheep, Human child, Cabbage, Cabbage white caterpillar, Robin, Hawk

Children need to understand the relationships within a food chain and to begin to think about the part that humans play in some of them. They need to know that almost all food chains start with a green plant and that the Sun is the ultimate source of all our energy. Plants are able to make food using this energy and this provides the starting point for transferring energy from species to species through food chains.

Discussing the photographs

▶ Create three slideshows of the photographs in each chain. Show these to the children and discuss the relationships between the organisms in each food chain. For instance, talk about how far more caterpillars are needed to feed a robin than robins to feed a hawk.

▶ Point out how some food chains may be longer than others. For example, the chain to get from cabbage to hawk is longer than the other two food chains.

▶ Discuss how, within these food chains, some species are both prey and predator. For instance, the robin and the caterpillar are both prey and predator.

▶ Talk about the effects of disruption in a food chain. For example, how a lack of insects in the spring can affect the number of blue-tit chicks that are reared, or if pesticides are used extensively on greenfly it could affect the number of ladybirds.

▶ Talk about the effects that humans can have on food chains, eg the use of weed killers or slug pellets. Can the children suggest ways to reduce human impact on food chains?

Activities

▶ As a class devise the shortest food chain you can think of. For example, wheat – person.

▶ Devise the longest food chain you can think of. Is there one longer than cabbage – hawk? (Rose, greenfly, ant, ant-eating bird, bird of prey.)

▶ Give the children a copy of the photographs in all the food chains and ask them to sort the photographs into food chains. Can they be sorted in different ways?

▶ Give the children a copy of the 'Food chain word cards' on photocopiable page 17, and ask them to label each organism in the three food chains they have created with *predator* or *prey*. What do they notice? (Some organisms need both labels.)

▶ Divide the class into two. Ask them to prepare a debate on the need for the increase in crop production to help feed the world versus the adverse effects of using pesticides.

▶ Show the children how to use a modelling programme on the computer to model the effects of disruption in a food chain.

IN THEIR HABITAT

Wading birds, Seaweed in sea, Bluebells in wood

Children should understand that living things are adapted to their habitats. For example, they may be able to move and breathe under water or fly in the air, they may be able to exist for long periods in very arid or wet conditions. Some animals can also digest food materials that would be poisonous to others and can, therefore, live in habitats that would not be suitable for other animals.

These photographs will introduce children to habitats they might not find in their locality. Wading birds live near water where they feed on small creatures. Their long legs enable them to wade into shallow water to search for their prey in its habitat. Seaweed can extract the nutrients it needs from seawater, although it still needs light in order to photosynthesise and produce its own food, so it cannot live at great depths. Some seaweeds grow to great lengths without rigid stems because they are supported by the water. Deciduous woodlands provide a habitat for bluebells that are adapted to grow and blossom early in the year before the canopy of leaves in the wood restricts their light too much.

Discussing the photographs

▶ Show the children the photograph 'Wading birds' and discuss how they are adapted to their habitat. Look at their long legs that allow them to wade through the shallow water, and the long beaks that enables them to search for small water creatures on which to feed.

▶ Look at 'Seaweed in sea' and discuss how seaweed is adapted to live in water. Explain how it uses the water to support its fronds, rather than developing rigid stems.

▶ Look at the photograph 'Bluebells in wood'. Talk about how the bluebells prefer an environment that provides dappled shade and how they flower before the trees come into full leaf and block out most of the sunlight.

▶ Ask the children to suggest other animals that have adapted to their habitats. For example, the otter has a streamlined shape that enables it to move through the water with little resistance, and has webbed feet to aid its swimming; the shape of a pike is also streamlined to enable it to move well in water and its colouring helps to camouflage it so that it can lie in wait for its prey.

Activities

▶ Ask the children to make an information sheet or leaflet about a specific organism, noting particularly how it is adapted to its habitat.

▶ Build a class diorama of a particular habitat, showing the plants and animals found there.

▶ As a class, make a detailed survey of a particular habitat, noting the range and frequency of flora and fauna found there.

▶ Give the children the puzzle sheet 'Where might it live?' (photocopiable page 21) to identify different habitats.

▶ Ask the children to use the Internet to find out about plants that grow in very different conditions, such as deserts or swamps. Ask them to focus on finding out how they are adapted to very dry, wet or cold conditions.

▶ Get the children to research how humans provide artificial habitats in order to grow crops out of season, or in different climatic conditions, to those of the plant's natural habitat. For example, how are crops grown in the desert? What makes greenhouses so useful?

▶ Ask the children to find out how genetic modification can make plants more drought tolerant or resistant to herbicides used to kill weeds. Prepare a class debate for and against genetic modification.

HABITATS

Seashore, River, Woodland

These photographs reinforce children's understanding that there are an enormous variety of habitats to which the flora and fauna living in them are adapted. They also lead to discussions and work on other, contrasting habitats, and on the need for humans to be aware of their impact on such habitats and the effects of pollution.

The seashore, at first glance, looks like a rather barren environment, trapped between the sea and the land. It is salty, and wet and dry by turns. But it is home to many living things. Sand fleas or razor shells, and rag worms are buried in the sand. Shellfish, such as limpets, can be found stuck to rocks. Crabs and other small creatures hide among the small seaweeds in rock pools when the tide goes out so that they do not dry out before the tide comes in again. Many of the creatures that live on the seashore are adapted to be immersed in seawater when the tide comes in, and exposed to the air when the tide goes out. This process is a cycle of about eight hours. The grass growing on the dunes plays an important part in preventing the erosion of the seashore. Its roots help to anchor the sand and prevent it being eroded by wind and water.

Rivers and their banks provide a home for both plants and animals. Many types of fish can be found in this habitat, the variety depending on the type of river. Clear, fast-flowing chalk streams will be home to trout, while perch and chub prefer slower moving waters. Fish, freshwater shellfish, freshwater crayfish, and so on, provide food for otters. Water voles make their nests in the riverbanks. Small creatures, such as mayflies and some species of dragonflies, find shelter in marginal plants and water weed. They lay their eggs in the water where the nymphs often spend time before emerging as adults.

The woodland photograph shows deciduous trees that lose their leaves in winter. This type of woodland provides a very rich habitat. The trees give both shelter and food to a large number of creatures, ranging from mammals, such as squirrels or deer, to birds and insects. Plants, such as bluebells, are adapted to living in such woodlands. Bluebells like dappled shade and grow and flower early before the canopy is too dense and blocks out the light they need. Fungi grow on dead and rotting wood, helping to break it down and return the nutrients it contains to the soil.

Discussing the photographs

▶ Look at the photographs with the children and ask if they can identify each habitat. Can they tell you the names of some of the creatures that are adapted to living in each one?

▶ Talk about any important plants or animals that the children have not mentioned and discuss each of the habitats in some detail. Explain how the flora and fauna in each are adapted to their habitat. For example, look at the 'River' photograph and talk about how fish are adapted to take oxygen from the water through their gills. Look at the 'Seashore' photograph and talk about how limpets can seal themselves to a rock on the seashore to avoid drying out between high tides, or discuss the fact that seaweeds can tolerate a high level of salt that would kill garden plants.

▶ Look at each photograph again and ask the children to compare the three habitats. Get them to look for similarities and differences. Ask questions, such as *Are there plants in each habitat? Does each habitat provide shade or shelter? Why can no animals be seen?*

▶ Ask the children if they know why it is important to care for the environment and avoid polluting the habitats in which creatures and plants live. For example, talk about how if contaminants of any kind get into a river they will kill the fish and other creatures that live there. Other creatures, such as otters, will be deprived of their food source. Explain that if woodland is subjected to pollutants, such as acid rain from manufacturing processes, the trees begin to die, and the shelter and food of all the creatures that depend on the trees diminishes and, therefore, the creatures themselves will decline. Discuss how oil washed up on seashores kills both the animals and plants that come into close contact with it.

▶ Talk about how important it is not to damage any habitats that the children visit. Explain that if everyone took a few pebbles home from the beach (which is illegal), there would soon be none left!

Activities

▶ As a class, use the Internet or other sources of information to find out in detail about each type of habitat depicted in the photographs. Make a class reference book for each one.

▶ Arrange a class visit to one or more of the types of habitat in the photographs. Take the class reference book for that particular habitat, made in the activity above, with you and see if the children can find and identify any of the species detailed in it.

▶ Get the children to compare the habitat the class visited, or one of the habitats in the photographs, with a different, local habitat. Are there any species in it that are the same? If so why? Are the conditions similar? Can the children identify any species in their local environment that would not be able to live in the habitat they visited, or vice versa? Ask the children to write a report of their findings.

▶ Organise the class to make posters or notices to help prevent damage to a local habitat, or the school environment. For example, notices asking people to take their litter home with them, or not to pick wild flowers or break the branches off trees.

NOTES ON THE PHOTOCOPIABLE PAGES

Word cards
PAGES 15–17

These word cards contain some of the basic vocabulary for the children to use and learn when looking at 'Interdependence and adaptation'. These include:
▶ words and sentences associated with plant growth
▶ words associated with food chains
Ask the children to read through the words and identify any they do not understand.
▶ Use the cards as a word bank to help the children label pictures or to help them with their writing.
▶ Read some of the words to the children and ask them to give you a definition.
▶ Give the children a definition and ask them to provide the word from the cards.
▶ Ask the children to look up any unfamiliar words in a dictionary and make a glossary.

Make your own liquid fertiliser
PAGE 18

This sheet takes the children through the steps involved in making their own liquid fertiliser. Remind the children before they start that fertiliser does not 'feed' plants, but only supplies the nutrients that enable plants to make their own new material for growth and repair. Talk about how plant material rots down and returns the nutrients to the earth to be used again. When the children have made their fertiliser they can devise a fair test to assess the optimum dilution of the fertiliser.

The children should be closely supervised when cutting and drilling and they may need help with this part of the worksheet.

Plants need...
PAGE 19

This is a recording sheet to use when investigating three plots of grass on the school field. Before the children embark upon the investigation, remind them what they have learned about the needs of plants for healthy growth.

Key questions
PAGE 20

This sheet provides a template for making an identification key. The children can use copies of it to record their questions when devising a key to identify organisms.

Where might it live?
PAGE 21

This is a puzzle sheet. Some children may be able to identify the creature, but they should all be able to work out the sort of habitat that would suit it and explain why. Ask the children to read through the first set of statements and make sure they understand what they need to do to complete the sheet. When the children have completed the sheet discuss the variety of habitats in which animals live.

water

light

warmth

nutrients

fertiliser

Plants need light to grow.

Plants need warmth to grow.

Plants need water to grow.

Food chain word cards

food chain

predator

prey

organism

producer

consumer

Make your own liquid fertiliser

You will need
• Two large empty plastic bottles, with caps
• A small piece of muslin or cling film
• A sharp knife
• A hand drill

What to do
1. Mark a line around one of the bottles 5cm below the shoulder.
2. Using a sharp knife, and great care, cut the top from the bottle around the line – ask your teacher for help if needed.
3. Drill one or two small holes in the cap of the second bottle – your teacher will help you with this.
4. Mark a line around the second bottle 5cm from the base and cut this portion off.
5. Turn this bottle upside down and place it inside the first bottle to make a column.
6. Place vegetable waste in the top of the column. NEVER put meat or animal products in your column.
7. Cover the open top of the bottle with muslin or cling film (make a few small holes if you use cling film).
8. Make sure the vegetable matter remains damp.

▶ Make several columns and fill each with different vegetable waste.

▶ Observe for the next few weeks.
Which kind of plant material rots down best?

▶ Experiment with the liquid fertiliser you have made. It will be very strong if taken straight from the column. Dilute it with water.

▶ Grow some cress and find out which is the best dilution of fertiliser to use.

Plants need...

▶ Set up an investigation into the conditions needed for healthy plant growth. Record your observations each week.

▶ Write an explanation of the results of your investigation in the appropriate plot.

Plot 1 (Covered in black plastic)

Week 1 _____

Week 2 _____

Week 3 _____

Week 1 _____

Week 2 _____

Week 3 _____

Plot 2 (Watered with fertiliser)

Plot 3 (Control)

Week 1 _____

Week 2 _____

Week 3 _____

Key Questions

► Write your question in the box to divide each group in two.

Yes	**No**

Yes	**No**

Where might it live?

I have four legs
I like my skin to be moist at all times
I can breathe through my skin
I like to lay my eggs in water

I am a _____
My ideal habitat would be _____
because _____

I like to be in the air
I feed on nectar and pollen
I need to keep warm to remain active

I am a _____
My ideal habitat would be _____
because _____

I like to be warm
I have to soak up the sun each morning before I become active
I don't like getting wet
I eat insects
I sometimes have to hide so that I am not eaten

I am a _____
My ideal habitat would be _____
because _____

I don't like the light
My eyes are not very good but I always know exactly where I am
The things I like to eat come out at night
I have wings but I'm not very good at walking

I am a _____
My ideal habitat would be _____
because _____

▶ Devise some more puzzles of your own for a friend to finish.

MICRO-ORGANISMS

Content and skills

This chapter links to unit 6B, 'Micro-organisms', of the QCA Scheme of Work for science at Key Stage 2. The Resource Gallery on the CD-ROM, together with the teacher's notes and photocopiable pages in this chapter, can be used when teaching this unit.

As with the QCA Scheme of Work, this chapter helps children to learn about micro-organisms and how they may be harmful or beneficial. They learn about the part some micro-organisms play in food production and how others may cause illness or decay. They learn that these organisms are living things and can feed, grow and reproduce.

The teacher's notes suggest ways of using the resources on the CD-ROM as a whole class, for group work or with individual children. Some of the activities suggested will link with other areas of the curriculum, such as English, maths, history or art. Wherever possible the activities encourage the children to ask questions and thus develop an enquiring approach to their learning.

Resources on the CD-ROM

The CD-ROM includes a photograph of a child who has measles, and another photograph shows tooth cavities caused by bacteria. A photograph of a child cleaning her teeth and another of a child washing their hands, helps to reinforce the fact that we are responsible for keeping ourselves as healthy as possible and the part that hygiene plays in eliminating harmful bacteria.

The CD-ROM contains an interview with a doctor. This gives information about the importance of immunisation to help prevent us catching some diseases and how this can also help to stop the spread of disease.

Photographs of mouldy bread and a mouldy apple show how micro-organisms help to break down vegetable matter so that the nutrients may be re-used. Microscopic images of yeast and e-coli give children the opportunity to learn about the structure and form of some microbes. Photographs of cheese-making show how micro-organisms are used in food production.

Photocopiable pages

The photocopiable pages in the book are also provided in PDF format on the CD-ROM and can be printed out from there. They include:
▶ word cards containing the essential vocabulary for the unit
▶ an information/worksheet on the importance of clean water
▶ biographies of scientists

Science skills

Teaching this unit using the CD-ROM and accompanying teacher's notes requires the children to draw upon a variety of skills. These include observing, questioning, finding out, describing, sorting, sequencing, listening, speaking, reading, writing and drawing. For example, finding out about the scientific discoveries of such people as Edward Jenner or Louis Pasteur will encourage research skills. Watching bread go mouldy will help to encourage observation skills and the keeping of careful records. Watching an interview with a doctor will encourage listening skills.

NOTES ON THE CD-ROM RESOURCES

WHAT MAKES PEOPLE ILL?

Child with measles, Mouth showing cavities, Child cleaning teeth, Child washing hands

At this stage some children may not distinguish between infectious diseases and other illnesses and conditions. It is important that children understand that not all illnesses are 'catching' so those classmates who may have other conditions, such as excema or asthma, are treated sensitively.

Children need to know that the terms germ or microbe are sometimes used instead of micro-organism to describe small living things that can be beneficial or can cause disease. The photographs of children with measles and tooth cavities can be used to lead to a discussion on organisms that cause illness and decay. The photographs of a child cleaning their teeth and washing their hands are starting points for talking about how careful hygiene can help to stop harmful micro organisms causing illness and decay.

Discussing the photographs

▶ Look at the photographs 'Child with measles' and 'Mouth showing cavities' and explain to the children what each one shows.

▶ Ask the children if any of them has ever had measles, or another serious illness, such as mumps. Can they describe how they felt and what happened to them? Have any of them had to have a tooth filled?

▶ Explain that many diseases are caused by micro-organisms. Talk about how, once inside the body, micro-organisms multiply and produce poisons (toxins) as waste products that make us ill. Tell the children that other terms for micro-organisms can be germ or microbe.

▶ Explain to the children that diseases such as measles, mumps and rubella are all caused by viruses and are infectious – that is, they can be passed from one person to another. Explain that tooth cavities, although caused by bacteria, are not infectious.

▶ Tell the children that bacteria, viruses and some fungi are so small that they cannot be seen by the human eye.

▶ Show the children the photograph 'Child cleaning teeth' and remind them about dental hygiene. Explain that harmful bacteria are present in the mouth, even though they cannot be seen. Reiterate to the children that regular brushing removes this harmful bacteria.

▶ Look at the photograph 'Child washing hands' and talk about general cleanliness and hygiene, and how washing with soap and water helps to get rid of harmful micro-organisms on the skin. Explain that this can prevent us catching some illnesses, such as stomach upsets.

▶ Discuss how other serious diseases, such as tubercolosis, can be prevented by vaccination or immunisation. Ask if any of the children have been immunised. Have they ever had injections before going on holiday?

▶ Explain that not all diseases are infectious. Tell the children that some people are born with certain conditions, such as a hearing or sight impairment, and some illnesses are caused when a part of the body fails to function properly, such as diabetes. Explain that these illnesses cannot be caught. Some more serious diseases are not easily caught and can only be passed from one person to another under certain conditions. For example, tuberculosis and leprosy need relatively long contact with an infected person before they can be passed on. Any discussion on sexually transmitted diseases should be in line with the school's policy on sex education.

▶ Discuss the fact that there are useful bacteria found in the gut and how these help to digest food and keep us healthy.

▶ Talk to the children about the useful bacteria used in the food industry to make bread, cheese and yogurt. Also about the part played by yeast in the brewing industry.

Activities

▶ Give the children a copy of the Health and disease word cards (1) and (2) on photocopiable pages 29 and 30, and copies of the photographs. Ask them to write a short piece about how diseases and infections are spread and how they can be prevented, using the word cards to help them with the salient vocabulary.

▶ Ask the children to find out how diseases are spread. For example, coughing and sneezing, dirty water, and so on.

▶ Ask the children to find out why clean drinking water is so important. Give them a copy of 'Clean water' (photocopiable page 31) to read and ask them to answer the questions.

▶ Ask the children to make posters to encourage people to wash their hands after going to the lavatory or before handling food.

▶ Ask the children to find out how malaria is spread. Ask them to focus on why it is proving so difficult to eradicate in spite of worldwide efforts (mosquitoes develop immunity to insecticides used on them and continue to breed). What effect might global warming have?

Interview with GP

Children need to understand that immunisation is done to stop them from catching various diseases, such as mumps and measles. Also that it is through immunisation that previously devastating diseases, such as smallpox, have been eradicated throughout the world. The doctor in the video explains the process of immunisation in a way in which the children can easily understand. Some children are very frightened of injections, and some may also associate all injections with taking recreational drugs. The video can be used to reassure children about injections, and to reinforce the idea that some injections are beneficial.

Discussing the interview

▶ Watch the video with the children and ask them to tell you some of the diseases that we can be immunised against.

▶ Ask the children why it is a good thing to be immunised against certain diseases. Can they remember what the doctor in the video said about this?

▶ Play the video again and focus on the part where the doctor talks about the beneficial effects for the community and the world of people being immunised against diseases. Can the children remember the disease that has been eradicated throughout the world through immunisation? (Smallpox.)

▶ Talk to the children about how the immunisation process works. Use the doctor's explanation on the video if you wish, where he talks about how antibodies work.

▶ Ask the children to tell you if any of them have been immunised. Can they remember what they were immunised against? Can they tell the class what happened? Did they get a sticker afterwards? Use the story, or the video, to reassure the children about injections. Point out the beneficial effects of being immunised and that, for the sake of a small needle prick, the benefits are well worth it.

▶ Discuss what the doctor in the video says about immunisation before going on holiday. Can the children remember which diseases he talked about that we don't have in this country? Have any of the children been immunised before going on holiday?

▶ Use the video to discuss the beneficial use of injections as opposed to the use of syringes for drug abuse. (Any such discussion must be in line with the school policy on drugs education.) Remind the children that they should never touch any syringes they might find and that they should tell an adult at once.

Activities

▶ Ask the children to find out about some of the scientists who discovered micro-organisms or ways of preventing disease. (Use the information sheets on Edward Jenner (photocopiable page 32), Louis Pasteur (photocopiable page 33) and Lady Mary Wortley-Montagu (photocopiable page 34) if appropriate.)

▶ In groups, ask the children to find out about, and prepare a presentation on, times in history when there were great epidemics. For example, the Great Plague, the Black Death or the influenza pandemic of 1918. Ask them to consider why these diseases spread so far and so quickly. For example, in the case of the influenza pandemic, soldiers returning from the First World War carried it home with them and infected their local populations.

▶ Invite a nurse into the classroom to talk more about personal hygiene, immunisation and disease prevention. This may link with the school's programme for personal, social and health education.

▶ Ask the children to write a piece about when injections are beneficial and when not. (Bear in mind the school's policy on drugs education.)

ROTTING

Mouldy apple, Mouldy bread

Microscopic organisms, such as moulds, can be seen by the human eye when they form colonies, as can some bacteria. Some bacteria are very important in the process of decay and returning nutrients to the earth for recycling. The photographs of the mouldy apple and mouldy bread show how mould spores can colonise things and help the process of decay.

It is easy to grow moulds on bread or fruit and most of these are not dangerous. However, when using moulds in the classroom they should be kept in sealed containers and disposed of without opening. Some children may have an allergic reaction to the spores given off. (See Be Safe published by ASE for more information.) Never use meat products in investigations of this type. Micro-organisms grown on meat can be very dangerous.

Discussing the photographs

▶ Look at the photographs with the children and ask them to describe what they show.

▶ Explain that decomposition is caused by micro-organisms. Talk about microbes helping to keep the world tidy. What would it be like if nothing ever rotted or decomposed?

▶ Explain to the children how nutrients from decomposing material return to the earth to nourish new growth. For example, compost heaps.

▶ Talk about how most moulds are visible, but other micro-organisms may not be, even though they are present in large numbers. Organisms that cause an upset stomach or food poisoning, for instance, may be present on our hands even though we cannot see them. Discuss the importance of washing hands after using the toilet or before handling food.

▶ Talk about how important it is for food shops to be clean. Ask the children why they think assistants need to wear overalls or aprons? Why do they wear hats or hair nets? Why do some wear plastic gloves?

▶ Discuss the importance of storing food safely. Talk about how meat, fish and cheeses need to be kept cool and covered. Explain that this is to stop them being contaminated by things such as flies and to slow down their deterioration. Talk about the significance of sell-by dates on food labels.

▶ Talk about the importance of cooking food thoroughly to destroy any micro-organisms that may be present in fish or meat prior to eating them.

Activities

▶ Collect (clean or washed) wrappings from different foods for the children to look at. Ask them to identify the sell-by or eat-by dates. Which foods keep for the shortest time and which the longest?

▶ Plan and carry out a fair test with the class to find out how to keep bread fresh for the longest time. For example, experiment with slices of bread in sealed plastic bags in the fridge, in a tin, on a plate on the window sill, and so on. Which goes mouldy first? Why? Get the children to describe what happens to each sample of bread in the test. (Dispose of the samples without unsealing them.)

▶ Leave an apple in a sealed container and ask the children to notice how long it takes to go rotten. They could keep a diary in words and pictures to record what happens.

▶ Make a compost heap in the school garden and ask the children to record what happens. Have they noted any things that don't decompose?

THROUGH THE MICROSCOPE

Yeast, E-coli

Micro-organisms are not classified as either plants or animals. Yeast is classified as a fungus.

Microscopes enable us to see things too small for the naked eye to be able to see. Yeast is a single cell organism that can multiply rapidly. There are many kinds of yeast and some are used in the food industry in baking or brewing. E-coli is a bacterium that can cause severe stomach upsets and even death in vulnerable people, such as the elderly and very young.

Discussing the photographs

▶ Talk to the children about how, long ago, people thought that a miasma – or a cloud of bad air – caused disease. Explain that after the invention of the microscope people discovered

'germs' and realised their importance and the part they played in causing disease.

▶ Explain that viruses are much smaller than bacteria and they weren't discovered until more powerful electron microscopes were available.

▶ Tell the children how some scientists, such as Joseph Lister, understood that disease could be passed from one person to another by infected material from wounds. He started to use a carbolic, or antiseptic, dressing while he was operating. He believed that this would kill the germs, even though he had never seen them.

▶ Look at the photographs with the children and ask if they know what they show. Explain that they show micro-organisms as seen under a microscope. One of the photos shows a disease-causing bacterium, E-coli, and the other shows a fungus, yeast. Explain to the children that E-coli can cause severe stomach upsets and even death in vulnerable people. Ask the children if they know how yeast is often used in the food industry.

Activities

▶ Look at an unwashed fingernail under a microscope with the class. Wash the finger and look again. Has all the dirt gone? Where is it still lurking? Try scrubbing and looking again.

▶ Ask the children to make a booklet telling people why cleanliness and hygiene in the kitchen are so important, and explaining that bacteria and viruses can't be seen by the naked eye.

▶ If possible, take the children to visit a hospital pathology department on an open day.

▶ Invite an Environmental Health Officer into school to talk about their work.

▶ Seal some bread into a clear jar and get the children to look for colonies other than green mould growing there. Dispose of the jar without opening when the investigation is over.

USEFUL BUGS

Separating curds and whey, Preparing the curd, Blue cheese

Children should understand that not all micro-organisms are harmful and that many are essential in keeping us healthy eg, bacteria in the gut are essential to digestion. Many micro-organisms are used in food production, to make food such as cheese or yogurt. The turning of milk into cheese is caused by micro-organisms effecting a chemical change in the consistency and taste of the milk. The blue veining in blue cheese is caused by a beneficial mould.

Discussing the photographs

▶ Discuss with the children the fact that micro-organisms are living things and that they need food and warmth in order to grow and reproduce, just as humans do.

▶ Show the photographs 'Separating curds and whey' and 'Preparing the curd'. Talk about cheese being the result of micro-organisms working in milk to change its taste and consistency. The first shows the start of the cheese-making process when rennet is added to the milk in order to start the process of separating the curds and whey. In the second, curd is being prepared before it is pressed into muslin-lined moulds for storing and ripening.

▶ Look at the photograph 'Blue cheese' and explain to the children how the blue veins are the result of an edible mould introduced into the cheese on copper wires.

▶ Explain to the children how yogurt is made: milk is inoculated with a micro-organism which reproduces, turning the milk to yogurt. These micro-organisms help to complement those found in the human gut and can help to keep us healthy.

▶ Talk about other microbes that are used in the food industry. Explain that the yeast used in baking is a micro-organism and that it can feed, grow and reproduce. Look at a piece of bread and explain how the holes are formed by the bubbles of gas (carbon dioxide) given off by the yeast as a waste product.

▶ Discuss with the children how yeast is used in the brewing industry and in fermenting wine.

Activities

▶ Carry out a class experiment with yeast. Mix a little yeast with tepid water in a small bottle and fix a balloon over the neck. Place the bottle in a warm place and get the children to observe it. Repeat the experiment, but add a small amount of sugar, and again ask the children to observe what happens. Ask them why they think more gas is given off when sugar is added to the mixture. (The yeast feeds on the sugar thus making more waste gas.)

▶ Let the children make bread dough with and without yeast and ask them to observe the difference in reactions.

▶ The children could make yogurt by adding a spoonful of live yogurt to a thermos flask of scalded and cooled milk in order to introduce the micro-organism that will change the whole flask of milk into yogurt. Leave overnight and let the children enjoy yogurt the next day.

SCIENTISTS

Edward Jenner, Louis Pasteur, Lady Mary Wortley-Montagu

These photographs are of three scientists who did a great deal to improve the health of people by discovering and recognising the part played by micro-organisms in causing and curing disease. These photographs can be used in conjunction with the information sheets on each of the scientists on photocopiable pages 32, 33 and 34.

Discussing the photographs
▶ Show the children the photograph of Edward Jenner and discuss the work he did in recognising that smallpox could be prevented by immunising against it.
▶ Look at the photograph of Louis Pasteur and discuss with the children how he recognised the part that bacteria played in making people ill, particularly from contaminated food such as milk. Explain how he discovered that many bacteria could be killed by heat.
▶ Lady Mary Wortley-Montagu was actually immunising people before Jenner but this was not made public possibly because, as a woman, she was not recognised as a scientist.

Activities
▶ Ask the children to research and write about other scientists, including those from other cultures, who have made discoveries that contribute to people's health.

NOTES ON THE PHOTOCOPIABLE PAGES

Word cards PAGES 20–30

These word cards contain some of the basic vocabulary for the children to use and learn when looking at the unit 'Micro-organisms'. Ask the children to read through the word cards. Are there any new or unfamiliar words that need clarifying?

Activities
▶ Use the word cards as a word bank to help the children label pictures or to aid their writing.
▶ Ask the children to look up any unfamiliar words in a dictionary and to make a glossary.
▶ Ask pairs of children to take turns to read out a word and the partner to give a definition.

Clean water PAGE 31

This sheet gives one example of how water can become contaminated and a simple solution to help prevent this.

Discussing the text
▶ Talk about the importance of having a supply of clean water with the children. Use the example on the sheet as an example of why contaminated water is not safe for consumption.
▶ Can the children think of any other examples of how water could become contaminated? For example, people using rivers for washing and waste disposal, run off from farm land.
▶ Talk about areas of the world where a clean water supply cannot be taken for granted. Discuss some of the diseases, such as cholera and typhoid, that are spread by dirty water.

Activities
▶ In groups, let the children experiment with a filter column to filter muddy water. Fill the column with layers of fine sand, then coarser sand, fine gravel, then coarser gravel. Cover the top of the column with some net or fine gauze. Show the groups how to pour muddy water in the top of the column and tell them to watch how the water at the bottom is cleaner. Talk about whether this water is really clean. Might there be things that we cannot see that

need treating in some other way? (Never drink the resulting water, however clean it looks.)
▶ As a class, find out what happens to the water we pour down the drain. Contact the local water company to either come in and talk to the children, or to send information to them.
▶ Encourage the children to contact charitable organisations, such as Water Aid, to find out what is being done to make sure everyone in the world has access to a clean water supply.

Edward Jenner

PAGE 32

Discussing the text
▶ Explain to the children that smallpox was a dreadful disease that killed or scarred a great many people, and that it was highly contagious.
▶ Talk about how Jenner made observations and then carried out experiments to prove his theories. Discuss how vaccination programmes have eradicated smallpox from the world.

Activities
▶ Show the children the photograph of Jenner from the Resource Gallery.
▶ Ask the children to find out about other diseases that are being targetted by the World Health Organisation (WHO), such as polio. Why is it important for such diseases to be controlled or eradicated?
▶ As a class, make a list of other diseases for which immunisation is available.

Louis Pasteur

PAGE 33

Discussing the text
▶ Talk about how people thought disease was caused before Pasteur discovered microbes.
▶ Discuss the ways in which Pasteur helped the brewing and wine-making industries.
▶ Ask: *How did Pasteur's work build on that of Jenner?*

Activities
▶ Show the photograph of Louis Pasteur from the Micro-organisms Resource Gallery.
▶ Ask the children to find out how milk is pasteurised. How do they think this process helped the health of people who drank milk?
▶ Take the children on a visit to a dairy to find out how dairy products are processed. Or use the cheese-making photographs from the Micro-organisms Resource Gallery, to show the children some of the stages involved in making cheese.
▶ Let the class make their own cream cheese. Allow a bottle of milk to go sour. (Leave it in a warm place so that the micro-organisms can get to work!) Strain the sour mixture through a clean muslin cloth or jelly bag until the whey has all drained away. Use the resulting curd (cream cheese) to make sandwiches.

Lady Mary Wortley-Montagu

PAGE 34

Discussing the text
▶ Discuss reasons why Jenner, rather than Lady Mary, was credited with introducing vaccination. (At that period in history, women were not thought to be capable of higher learning and scientific thought and were, therefore, not credited with any discoveries they made. Lady Mary was only able to influence close friends and doctors because of her high position in society.)
▶ Talk about the benefits of vaccination with the children. Discuss the diseases they are likely to have been vaccinated against, such as polio, measles, tuberculosis.

Activities
▶ Ask the children to research other women scientists who have made important discoveries in the health field and to make a glossary of these.
▶ Ask the children to find out when women were first allowed to become doctors. Who was the first woman doctor? (Elizabeth Garrett Anderson in 1865.)

Health and disease word cards (1)

immunisation

vaccination

micro-organisms

germ

microbe

bacteria

Health and disease word cards (2)

virus

infectious

tooth decay

hygiene

cleanliness

Clean water

Many people in developing countries rely on wells for their water supply.

These may be simple holes in the ground.

Animals may be kept in the same field as the well.

Animal dung and urine may be washed or trampled into the well. Small animals may fall into the well. These things would cause the water to become contaminated.

Simply building a wall around the edge of the well could prevent this contamination and create a healthier community.

Finding out about clean water

1. Find out what is being done to ensure that everyone in the world has access to clean drinking water.

2. Write to some of the aid agencies to find out what they are doing to provide clean water around the world.

3. Make a leaflet explaining why it is so important to use clean water.

4. Find out about some of the diseases that are carried in water.

© IMAGESTATE

Edward Jenner (1749–1823)

Edward Jenner trained as a doctor in London. He spent some time as an army surgeon before becoming a country doctor in Gloucestershire.

In those days, smallpox was a dreaded disease. It killed many people and those who did recover were often dreadfully scarred. Jenner noticed that milkmaids were catching a disease from the cows they milked, called cowpox. This was a mild infection from which people recovered very quickly. Jenner also noticed that the milkmaids who had cowpox did not get smallpox.

Jenner wanted to test out his observations. In May 1796, Sarah Nelmes consulted Jenner about a rash on her hand. He diagnosed cowpox and decided to experiment. He used some of the material from the blisters on Sarah's hand to infect someone who had not yet had smallpox, with cowpox.

Jenner chose as his subject James Phipps, the eight-year-old son of his gardener. He made a few scratches on James's arm and rubbed in some of the material from one of the blisters on Sarah's arm. A few days later James developed cowpox, but was soon quite well again. Jenner now knew that cowpox could be passed from person to person, as well as from cow to person. The next step was fairly drastic. Jenner inoculated the boy with smallpox and, much to his relief, James did not develop smallpox. This was almost 100 years before people realised that disease was caused by microbes.

Jenner followed this experiment with many more. He was able to show quite clearly that having cowpox protected people from the much more serious disease of smallpox. However, people still did not understand about microbes and how they could spread disease.

Vaccination took quite a long time to become an accepted practice. At first, the cowpox material often became contaminated with smallpox, since those administering it often worked in smallpox hospitals. Since microbes were unknown, the need for cleanliness was not understood and many people were infected with smallpox along with cowpox. Also, cowpox material was not available all over the country.

Jenner spent much of the rest of his life supplying cowpox material to countries all over world so that their populations could be vaccinated against the deadly disease. In 1853, after Jenner had died, vaccination became compulsory, despite protests from those who wanted the right to choose. In 1980, the World Health Assembly declared that the world was free of smallpox.

Louis Pasteur (1822–1895)

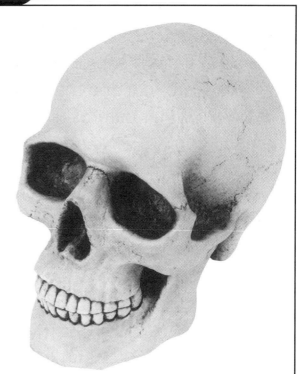

Louis Pasteur was born in 1822 in the Jura region of France. At that time people did not understand how diseases were caused and passed from person to person. It was thought that miasmas, or bad air, caused disease. People believed that life could arise spontaneously in organic materials.

Pasteur discovered that most infectious diseases were, in fact, caused by germs. He also discovered that some organisms could exist without oxygen and this led to the study of germs that cause gangrene and septicaemia.

He became very interested in the process of brewing, and his observations led him to believe that micro-organisms were involved in the fermentation process. He demonstrated that wine diseases caused by microbes, which were causing considerable loss to the wine industry, could be killed by heating the wine to 55°C for several minutes. He found that the same process could be applied to beer and even milk. 'Pasteurisation' was soon used throughout the world. This was a great benefit to health, since diseases passed on through unpasteurised milk, such as tuberculosis, caused many deaths.

In 1865, Pasteur began to study diseases in the silkworm and discovered the microbes that were causing them. He found out how they were transmitted and, very importantly, how they could be stopped. Calling on his work in brewing and wine-making he was able to show that each disease was caused by a specific microbe. Using this knowledge, Pasteur was able to establish some basic rules of asepsis and sterilisation in preventing the spread of disease and infection.

He developed vaccines against diseases such as rabies, anthrax, chicken cholera, and silkworm diseases, and laid the basis for immunisation. He found that weakened forms of a microbe could help fight infection by more virulent forms.

Pasteur pioneered changes to hospital practices in preventing infection that remain cornerstones of medicine even today.

© INGRAM PUBLISHING

Lady Mary Wortley-Montagu 1689– 1762

Lady Mary was born into a wealthy family in the late seventeenth century. In those days girls were not educated as boys were, but she managed to educate herself by reading the books in her parents' library. She even managed to teach herself Latin.

In 1712, Lady Mary eloped with and married Edward Wortley-Montagu, and in 1714 her husband was appointed Ambassador to Turkey. Lady Mary was fascinated by all things Turkish. She learned the language and spent a great deal of time meeting Turkish women and learning their customs.

When she returned to England she introduced the Turkish custom of inoculating children with a weakened strain of smallpox which gave them immunity from the more virulent strains of the disease. Lady Mary knew very well about smallpox. She herself had had the disease in 1715, and her brother had died from it. She had her son inoculated while they were in Turkey and three years later returned to Istanbul to have her baby daughter inoculated.

She managed to persuade some of her friends who were doctors about the benefits of inoculation, and many of her high society friends followed her lead in having their children inoculated.

Inoculation at that time was an expensive business and ordinary, poor people could not afford it. Later, Edward Jenner was given credit for introducing a smallpox vaccine that reached a wider population.

MORE ABOUT...
DISSOLVING/REVERSIBLE AND IRREVERSIBLE CHANGES

Content and skills

This chapter links to units 6C and 6D of the QCA Schemes of Work for science at Key Stage 2. The Dissolving/Reversible and Irreversible Changes Resource Gallery on the CD-ROM, together with the teacher's notes and photocopiable pages in this chapter, can be used when teaching this unit.

As with the QCA Scheme of Work, this chapter reinforces and extends the children's understanding of physical and chemical changes and the difference between them. They are encouraged to be aware of the potential hazards associated with some household chemicals and materials, and to recognise hazard warnings.

The teacher's notes suggest ways of using the resources as a whole class, for group work or with individual children. Some of the activities suggested will link with other areas of the curriculum, such as English, maths, ICT or history. Wherever possible the activities encourage the children to ask questions and develop an enquiring approach to their learning.

Resources on the CD-ROM

The CD-ROM includes photographs of cooked and uncooked food, melting chocolate, and so on, to lead work on physical and chemical changes and understanding the difference between them. Images of hazard labels help children to understand that there are dangers associated with some of the things that we use every day. A video and photographs of fuels burning reinforce ideas about chemical changes and the understanding that when things have burnt the change is irreversible and that new substances are made.

Photocopiable pages

The photocopiable pages in the book are also provided in PDF format on the CD-ROM and can be printed out from there. They include:
▶ word cards containing the essential vocabulary of the unit
▶ work sheets on defining physical or chemical changes, and recognising hazards.

Science skills

Skills such as observing, questioning, researching, describing, sorting, sequencing, listening, speaking, reading and writing are involved in the activities in the teacher's notes suggested for the unit. For example, holding a class debate on the pros and cons of clearing rainforests will develop the children's researching, speaking and listening skills. Conducting an experiment to make nails rust will encourage their observation and writing skills.

NOTES ON THE CD-ROM RESOURCES

MAKING IT CLEAN

Sewage plant

Impurities that are suspended or dissolved in water have to be eradicated in order to make our drinking water safe, or to clean sewage water to enable us to return it into the water cycle. Children sometimes confuse the words 'suspended' and 'dissolved' and need to be clear as to the difference between them.

This photograph shows an example of impure water being made clean. It shows filter beds at a sewage plant where fine gravel is used to filter particles from the sewage that has already been partially treated. The filter beds remove matter from the sewage which is then broken down in the gravel by bacteria living there. The water that remains has its oxygen levels increased by boom pipes and will then be ready to flow into rivers that are close to the plant.

Discussing the photograph

▶ Look at the photograph and ask the children if they can tell you what it depicts. Explain that it shows a sewage plant and how the sewage is turned into water that is clean enough to be released back into rivers.

▶ Talk with the children about the need for pure water to drink.

▶ Ask the children to tell you what they remember about how the water cycle works from their studies in Year 5. Reiterate that the process is cyclical and that nothing comes in or goes out. Therefore, we are reusing water and it has to be made safe. So, for example, water from the sewage plant in the photograph needs to be clean enough to be returned to the water cycle.

▶ Ask the children if they can give you a definition of the difference between a 'suspension' (a solid whose particles are suspended in a liquid) and a 'solution' (a solid dissolved in a liquid). Remind them that not all substances dissolve.

▶ Talk with the children about the fact that we cannot see substances that are dissolved in water. Because they are intimately mixed, no visible particles remain and the liquid is clear, although it may have changed colour. Whereas, if a solid is suspended in a liquid, the particles are floating and the liquid remains cloudy. Explain that if a suspension is left for long enough, the particles will sink to the bottom of the liquid and form a layer.

▶ Tell the children that a liquid can have solids both dissolved and suspended in it at the same time and that the process of separation is different.

▶ Discuss how layers of gravel, sand and charcoal with graded particles that get finer and finer are used to filter and remove solids that are suspended in water. Talk about how evaporation is used to regain and remove dissolved solids.

▶ Explain to the children that chemicals are also used to kill microscopic living organisms, such as bacteria.

▶ Talk about how sanitation is vital in order to prevent the spread of disease through water and how many people on earth still do not have access to clean water.

Activities

▶ Take the children to visit a water or sewage works. The children should prepare some questions to ask in advance of the visit. (All visits should be undertaken with reference to the school policy on visits.)

▶ In groups, make a gravel/sand filter to get muddy water clean. A small mesh sieve over a basin would be suitable to make the filter in. Place layers of fine gravel, sand, muslin and charcoal in the sieve. Ask the children to look carefully at the water when it has been filtered. Is it still slightly coloured? Why? Are there still some fine particles in suspension in it, or is there a coloured substance that is dissolved? Let them find out by setting the water aside and allowing any particles in suspension to sink to the bottom. Is the water still coloured? They could find out if any solids are dissolved by evaporating the water, either by putting it in sunlight or on a warm radiator. (Beware – make sure the children do not drink or taste the water, even if it looks completely clear. It could still have impurities in it including bacteria, as it has not been chemically treated. Make sure that the muddy water used is unlikely to be contaminated by dog faeces too.)

▶ Ask the children to produce a flow chart to sequence the steps used to separate the mixture in the experiment above.

▶ In small groups, make a large collection of substances that do and don't dissolve in water. Ask the children to predict before trying whether they will dissolve or not. Are some substances, such as coffee grounds, both suspended and dissolved? What about substances made from more than one ingredient, such as bath salts?

▶ Use the 'Changes word cards (1)' on photocopiable page 42 and ask the children to write definitions of the words relating to separating mixtures.

▶ Ask the children to use the Internet and/or other secondary sources to find out about some of the effects of impure water getting into the water cycle, or about some of the diseases that are caused and spread by impure water.

EVAPORATING

Video: Water evaporating from a muddy footprint

This video shows water evaporating in a muddy footprint. Water evaporates from all bodies of water, including one as small as a footprint. The evaporated water rises into the atmosphere where it condenses into droplets, precipitates and falls as rain, hail, sleet or snow, depending on the temperature at the precipitation level. The process of evaporation then begins all over again. This cyclical process is called the water cycle.

Discussing the video

▶ Play the video to the children. Encourage them to tell you what is happening in it and to describe the process of evaporation.

▶ Ask the children to tell you what they remember about their work on evaporation from studies in Year 5.

▶ Talk about how heat and wind affect the rate at which evaporation occurs. Remind the children that evaporation occurs all the time, not just when it is hot. Explain that evaporation in low temperatures is very slow.

▶ Talk with the children about the commercial uses of evaporation, such as in the production of salt and in the distilling process.

▶ Remind the children that it is not just water that evaporates. All liquids evaporate if their liquid state is not maintained.

▶ Can the children tell you about any occurrences of evaporation, besides water, that they might encounter? For example, nail varnish, paint and wood varnish drying.

▶ Tell the children that when some substances evaporate the vapour that they produce can be dangerous. For example, petrol, where the vapours are flammable, and glue, where the vapours are toxic and are dangerous if sniffed.

Activities

▶ Make a strong solution of salty water and show the children how to reclaim the salt by evaporation. A sunny windowsill is suitable. If boiling the water to evaporate it, it is best not to boil the water away completely because the hot salt tends to spit. Make sure the children are kept well away from boiling water.

▶ Put a plastic beaker or tray of water covered with cling film in the sunshine or on a hot radiator. Let the children watch the evaporated water condense and fall back into the container as droplets of water.

▶ Ask the children to make annotated drawings and to write a definition of the condensation and evaporation process.

▶ Let the children evaporate the liquid from nail polish, paint, ink and any other safe liquid they suggest.

▶ Ask the children to make a fair test to show which liquid evaporates the quickest. For example, they could use water, nail polish, wood varnish, and so on, in measured amounts in the same conditions in the same type of container.

▶ Ask the children to find out where salt is produced in large commercial quantities – in this country and in other countries.

▶ Challenge the children to make a fair test to find out the quickest way to speed up the evaporation process. For example, they could soak pieces of cloth or paper towels of the same type and size in water for the same amount of time and then compare the drying time using different methods. For example, hanging them indoors, hanging them out in the sunshine or wind, using a fan, and so on.

▶ Suggest the children use the Internet or other reference sources to research and write an information leaflet about Ghandi and his protests about the salt tax in India.

CHANGES

Cake mixture in basin, Baked cake, Raw egg, Fried eggs, Uncooked bread dough, Baked loaves, Chocolate, Melted chocolate, Ice block, Melting ice cubes

Children need to know the difference between a physical change (one that can be reversed) and a chemical change (one that cannot be reversed and where a new substance is formed).

Some examples of a physical change are melting, freezing, evaporating, condensing and dissolving. The photographs 'Chocolate' and 'Melted chocolate' show a physical change that has taken place, as do the photographs 'Ice block' and 'Melting ice cubes'.

Some examples of chemical changes are burning, cooking, rusting, firing clay, and so on. The photographs 'Cake mixture in basin' and 'Baked cake', 'Raw egg' and 'Fried eggs', 'Uncooked bread dough' and 'Baked loaves' all show examples of a chemical change.

Discussing the photographs

▶ Discuss with the children the difference between physical and chemical changes. Explain that a physical change is one that can be reversed, and a chemical change is one that cannot be reversed and a new substance is made by the change. Talk through a few examples, asking the children to suggest some more.

▶ Tell the children that they are going to look at some photographs showing physical and chemical changes. Look at each of the photographs with the children and ask if they can identify the objects that pair together where a change has occurred, for instance the 'Raw egg' and 'Fried eggs' photographs. Can they tell you which changes are chemical and which are physical?

▶ Talk about the fact that irreversible changes are often, but not always, caused by the action of heat on a material. For example, a cake baking in the oven, a pot fired in a kiln or wood burning.

▶ Discuss examples of chemical changes not caused by the action of heat, such as rusting.

▶ Remind the children that a physical change can happen over and over again, such as melting and freezing water, or the changes in the water cycle that is a continuous process.

Activities

▶ Use the 'Changes word cards (2)' on photocopiable page 43 to familiarise the children with the important vocabulary for the unit.

▶. Give the children a copy of the 'Physical or chemical change?' sheet (photocopiable page 45) to identify the different changes. Ask them to think of more changes to add to the sheet and to

pass to their friends to sort into physical or chemical changes
▶ Let the children make cakes or bread, ensuring that they look closely at the changes at every stage of the process.
▶ Let the children make and fire clay pots. Ask them how many changes the pot has gone through. (When it is air-dried the pot is physically changed. Water can be added to the clay to make it plastic again. The fired pot is chemically changed and a new material has been formed. The adding of water will not make the clay plastic again.)
▶ Can the children suggest a way to make nails go rusty? For example, put the nails in a screw-top jar with some water. Make sure the children examine the nails every day to see the degree of rust. Keep some of the same type of nails dry in order to make comparisons. Talk about whether the nails can be made rust free again, or whether a chemical change has taken place.
▶ Let the children melt and freeze ice over and over again, to demonstrate that melting and freezing are physical changes that can be reversed.

WARNINGS

Hazard label (furniture), Hazard label (correction fluid)

All materials used domestically, from clothes and furniture to household and garden chemicals, have to carry a hazard warning label if they are potentially dangerous. Many hazards occur during the process of a physical or chemical change. For example, when fabric in clothes, or fabrics and foam in furniture, burn they can give off toxic fumes that are highly dangerous. There is also the possibility that people may be burned. Some aerosol sprays are dangerous if breathed in. Other chemicals are dangerous if swallowed or if they come into contact with the skin. These photographs show hazard labels from everyday items, which the children may not consider are made from potentially hazardous materials. They can be used to discuss safety in the home with children.

Discussing the pictures
▶ Look at the pictures with the children and ask them what they think the pictures tell them. Explain that it is not only things in bottles or cans that carry warning labels, but that furniture and clothes carry a warning against naked flames (although, if used correctly, there is not usually a problem).
▶ Look at the 'Hazard label (furniture)' picture with the children and mention that upholstered furniture has to be to the proper safety standards in terms of being made from fire retardant materials, but that it still has to carry a warning about keeping it away from fire.
▶ Talk about the fact that some materials are dangerous, in particular if misused, and that it is always wise to read the safety instructions or hazard warnings on clothes. Pyjamas and nighties, for example, usually warn the wearer to keep away from fire and children should be aware of this.
▶ Look at the 'Hazard label (correcton fluid)' picture and discuss the importance of reading instructions or warnings before using such substances including paint or super glue.

Activities
▶ Ask the children to look at home and list any clothing or furniture items that carry hazard labels. Why do they think the items they have listed carry warnings? Is it because of the material they are made from?
▶ Ask the children, when out shopping, to look for warning labels on new upholstered furniture and clothes, particularly nightwear, such as pyjamas.
▶ Make a collection of empty cans and containers and ask the children to look for any hazard warning that they carry. Make sure that containers are empty and have been washed out before allowing the children to handle them.
▶ Give the children a copy of the 'What is the symbol?' sheet (photocopiable page 46) and ask them to match the correct hazard symbol with its meaning.
▶ Use the sheet called 'What is the hazard?' (photocopiable page 47) for the children to record and note the substances they bring into class or find at home against the correct hazard label.
▶ Ask the children to find out how hazardous spills are dealt with, such as asbestos, oil, chemicals, radioactive material, and so on. Contact the local Fire service for information.

▶ Ask the children to find out about the nuclear accident at Chernobyl and its consequences. They could use the Internet or other reference sources.

BURNING

Gas hob with pan, Coal fire, Log fire, Barbeque, Fireworks
Video: Paper burning

Children need to understand that when something is heated its temperature is raised, but it is not set alight. When something burns it is set alight and a flame is seen, although some things, such as charcoal, burn with an almost invisible flame.

Burning, or combustion, is a chemical reaction with oxygen from the air and new substances are formed in the form of waste gas and, sometimes, ash.

Photograph © SODA

Discussing the resources

▶ Play the video of the paper burning and ask the children if they can tell you what is happening. Talk about the fact that there is a material (fuel) that is burning and that heat, light (flame) and waste substances (carbon dioxide gas and ash) are being produced.

▶ Play the video again and compile a slideshow of the photographs to show to the children. Can they name the fuel in each of the combustion processes? (Paper, gas, coal, wood, charcoal and various chemicals in fireworks.) Can they give you any other everyday examples of burning?

▶ Remind the children about the difference between burning and heating.

▶ Tell the children that although electricity, batteries, waves, water, wind, and so on, can be used as energy to produce, for example, heat and light, they are not fuels as no burning takes place.

▶ Discuss with the children how burning is a chemical change that cannot be reversed. Look together at the photographs and focus on each fuel that is burning and how it cannot be reversed.

▶ Discuss the fact that some substances made and given off during the burning process contribute to pollution in the atmosphere and global warming. For example, carbon dioxide, dioxins and carbon monoxide.

Activities

▶ Use the 'Burning word cards' on photocopiable page 44 to familiarise children with the important vocabulary.

▶ Ask the children to observe closely while a candle burns. Ask them to note what the fuel is in this combustion process (wax) and to note as many other observations as possible. How can the children tell that the wax (fuel) has been burnt during the process and that the change in the candle cannot be reversed? (Weigh the candle before burning and again afterwards to find how much wax has been consumed.)

▶ Make a collection of small pieces of different materials, such as paper, fabric and wood. Ask the children to observe closely as they burn and discuss what is made. For example, ash or smoke. Ask the children if they think that anything else is being made that they can't see. Talk about how they might know that a gas is being made – can they smell anything? (Only burn small pieces of the various materials and make sure that the children are at a safe distance.)

▶ Organise a class debate on the use of fossil fuels and the need for conservation. The children can used the Internet or other reference sources to prepare their notes.

▶ As a class, debate the pros and cons of the 'slash and burn' method of clearing rainforests. Ask some children to play the role of the people living in the area who need to clear the forest to grow crops to eat or to make money from. Another group of children could argue the conservationist case.

NOTES ON THE PHOTOCOPIABLE PAGES

Word cards

PAGES 42–44

These word cards contain some of the basic vocabulary for the children to use and learn when learning about the units More about dissolving and Reversible and irreversible changes. These include:
- ▶ words associated with separating mixtures
- ▶ words associated with changes
- ▶ words associated with burning.

Ask the children to read through the words and to give you definitions for some of them. Are there any words that the children don't understand?

Activities

- ▶ Place all the word cards randomly on a table and ask the children to sort them into themes.
- ▶ Ask the children to summarise their learning at the end of the unit by writing sentences on each theme using the word cards as pointers.

Physical or chemical change?

PAGE 45

This sheet will reinforce the children's ability to distinguish between a physical and a chemical change. It offers everyday processes for them to assess. Before they begin, ask the children to remind you of the difference between a physical and a chemical change. Can they give you some examples in each category? Ask the children to read through the sheet and make sure it is understood.

When they have completed the sheet, ask some of them to share the additional examples they thought of with the class.

You could also use the sheet for the children to play Snap or Matching Pairs games. Enlarge the statements on the sheet, cut them up and make them into cards (you will need several copies of each statement). To play, the children can collect pairs that are both a chemical change or a physical change. If the cards don't match they are put face down again for the next player's turn.

What is the symbol?

PAGE 46

This sheet helps children to recognise hazard symbols and what they mean. Before the children use the sheet, talk about how symbols enable us to quickly recognise the hazard associated with a particular substance or material. Read through all the definitions on the sheet with the children, if appropriate.

What is the hazard?

PAGE 47

This sheet encourages children to be aware that some everyday substances can be hazardous and to recognise the type of hazard that they could present.

The children could fill the sheet in at home or at school. If they are looking at home to find any household chemical labels, tell them to make sure that they have an adult with them.

melt

dissolve

suspension

solution

evaporate

condense

physical

chemical

freezing

melting

cooking

evaporating

fuel

combustion

burning

heating

Physical or chemical change?

▶ Put a P or C by each statement to show whether it is a physical or chemical change.

Change	P or C
Making ice	
Evaporating water	
Cooking a cake mixture	
Hard boiling an egg	
Freezing water	
Dissolving sugar in water	
Rusting a nail	
Burning wood	
Filtering dirty water	
Making concrete	
Dissolving salt	
Making egg custard	
Firing a pot in a kiln	
Making bread	
Melting chocolate	
Can you think of any other physical or chemical changes to add to the sheet? Ask your friends to sort them into P or C.	

45

What is the symbol?

▶ Cut up the sheet and match the correct symbols and descriptions.

	Highly flammable: These can be liquids, solids or gases. They catch fire very easily and should be kept well away from heat, flames or sparks.
	Radioactive: The dangerous rays these materials give off are invisible. They should always be locked away in special containers. Never touch them or even go near them.
	Oxidising agent: Because they contain a lot of oxygen these chemicals can help fires to burn. They should be kept well away from highly flammable materials.
	Harmful or irritant: These chemicals can be very dangerous if you get them on your skin, in your eyes or swallow them. Use water to wash them away as quickly as possible.
	Corrosive: These are strong acids or alkalis. They can damage your skin or your clothes if you spill them.
	Toxic: These chemicals are very poisonous. You must not get them on your hands or near your mouth. Never breathe in the vapour.
	Electric shock: High voltage electricity is very dangerous and a severe electric shock could kill you.
	Explosive: These chemicals are very dangerous. Heat, flame, a spark or even a sharp knock could make them explode.

What is the hazard?

▶ List the substance underneath its hazard warning symbol.

Toxic	Corrosive	Harmful or irritant	Highly flammable
Risk of electric shock	**Explosive**	**Oxidising agent**	**Radioactive**

Have you found some substances to list in every box?

If not why not?

◣ SCHOLASTIC
PHOTOCOPIABLE

READY RESOURCES ▶▶ S C I E N C E

FORCES IN ACTION

Content and skills

This chapter links to unit 6E, 'Forces in action', of the QCA Scheme of Work for science at Key Stage 2. The Resource Gallery on the CD-ROM, together with the teacher's notes and photocopiable pages in this chapter, can be used when teaching this unit.

As with the QCA Scheme of Work, this chapter reinforces and builds on what children have learned about forces in Key Stage 1 and 2. It will help children remember and learn more about how forces make things move, speed up, slow down, change direction and stop. It focuses children on the force of gravity and such things as magnetic force.

The teacher's notes include ways of using the resources as a whole class, for group work or with individual children. Some of the activities suggested will link with other areas of the curriculum, such as English, maths, history or art. Wherever possible the activities encourage the children to ask questions and develop an enquiring approach to their learning.

Resources on the CD-ROM

The CD-ROM includes photographs of an astronaut in a space suit, objects suspended from an elastic band and from a bar magnet, divers on high boards, a bungy jumper and a parachutist. These images can be used to lead children to discussions and activities related to the force of gravity. The image of the parachutist helps children to find out how friction, in the form of air resistance, can affect the speed at which things fall. The images also provide for work on the direction in which forces are acting and an understanding that forces usually act in pairs.

Photocopiable pages

The photocopiable pages in the book are also provided in PDF format on the CD-ROM and can be printed out from there. They comprise:
► word cards containing the essential vocabulary of the unit
► a work sheet on forces acting in pairs.

Science skills

Skills such as observing, questioning, researching, finding out, describing, listening, speaking, reading, writing and drawing are involved in the activities suggested in the teacher's notes that accompany the CD-ROM for the unit. For example, discussing forces and investigating their effects enables children to build on their speaking, listening and questioning skills, and on their ability to devise fair tests to find out more.

NOTES ON THE CD-ROM RESOURCES

GRAVITY AND OTHER FORCES

Astronaut on Moon, Astronauts in space, Weightlessness in spacecraft, Mug on elastic band, Paperclip on bar magnet, Divers, Bungy jumper, Parachutist

Forces are sometimes difficult for children to understand because they cannot see them, although they can see their effects. Children need to recognise that weight is a force measured in Newtons. (Mass is measured in kilograms.) It is not necessary for children to know the difference between weight and mass at this stage. However, some children find it fascinating and you may feel that it is appropriate to teach it. If so, you could explain to the children that mass is a measure of how much 'stuff' there is in an object and weight is the force of gravity acting on that mass.

Some children think that gravity only applies on Earth. They need to understand that all masses, including the Moon and other planets, have their own gravity. The astronaut in the photograph is experiencing the Moon's gravity, but because it is less than that on Earth he weighs less.

Children also often think that gravity just pulls down and don't realise that it pulls towards the centre of the Earth. The photographs of the mug suspended from an elastic band and the paperclip hanging from a bar magnet, show that gravity is pulling both objects down, but that the elastic band is exerting an upward force and the paper clip is being attracted by the magnetic force.

The photographs of the divers, bungy jumper and parachutist show people falling through the air. They are being pulled towards the centre of the Earth by gravity. Air resistance slows the rate at which they all fall to some extent. Upthrust by the water will slow the divers down even more. The parachute increases air resistance and slows the parachutist's fall to a rate at which he can land safely. The bungy cord is carefully calibrated to stop the bungy jumper's fall before he hits the ground.

Children need to recognise, and be able to describe, situations in which more than one force is acting on an object at the same time. They need to understand that forces usually act in pairs and are directional, but for practical purposes children need only identify the main forces acting.

Another common mistake that children often make is thinking that gravity does not act through liquid. They need to know that water has an upward force called upthrust that acts against the force of gravity.

Discussing the photographs

▶ Show the photographs to the children and ask if they can tell you the name of the force that is pulling things down in them.

▶ Discuss the fact that gravity is an invisible force that pulls things towards the centre of the Earth. Remind them that the force of gravity (weight) is measured in Newtons.

▶ Talk about the effects of gravity that the children can see in the photographs, in terms of falling objects. For example, the parachutist, the bungy jumper and the divers are being pulled down by gravity.

▶ Look at the photograph 'Divers' again with the children and talk about how they fall because gravity is pulling them down. Explain how, as they dive they make themselves into a streamlined shape to minimise both the air resistance and the upthrust of the water.

▶ Look together at the photographs 'Astronaut on Moon', 'Astronauts in space' and 'Weightlessness in spacecraft'. Remind the children that a body such as the Moon has a gravitational force. Because the Moon is smaller than the Earth its gravitational pull is only 1/6th of that of the Earth. Explain that this is why astronauts can take giant leaps on the Moon, because they weigh only 1/6th of what they weigh on Earth. Point out also that things are weightless in a spacecraft because of the lack of gravity in space.

▶ Tell the children that all objects actually fall at the same speed, but that they are slowed down by friction in the form of air resistance to a greater or lesser extent. For example, a parachute slows the parachutist down because of the air resistance on the large area of fabric.

▶ Tell the children that gravity also acts on and through liquids and that liquids are still being pulled towards the centre of the Earth.

▶ Ask the children if they have ever tried wading through water. Ask if it is as easy as walking on the ground. Why not? (Because the water is resisting your body.) Explain that this is a form of friction.

▶ Talk about the fact that water has an upwards force called *upthrust* and that this is why we feel lighter when in the water, because the water is exerting a force (upthrust) on us.

▶ Mention that gravity is not just a force found on Earth. All masses exert a gravitational force to a greater or lesser extent, depending on their mass.

▶ Look at the photographs again and ask the children to describe what is happening and how gravity is acting now that you have discussed how forces and gravity work in more detail.

▶ Talk about the fact that forces usually act in pairs. Look with the children at the photograph 'Paperclip on bar magnet' and explain that the force of gravity is trying to pull the paperclip down, while the magnetic force is holding it in place. Similarly, in the photograph 'Mug on elastic band', gravity is pulling the mug down while the elastic band is exerting an upward force.

▶ Focus on the photograph 'Bungy jumper'. Explain what is happening as the bungy jumper falls and why they stop before reaching the ground. (The force of gravity is pulling the jumper towards the centre of the Earth, but the elasticity of the bungy cord is carefully calibrated so that the drop is limited.)

Activities

▶ Ask the children to find out about Isaac Newton, after whom the Newton meter and the measure we use to find weight is named. The children could write an information sheet about him and his discovery, using the 'Forces word cards' on photocopiable page 53 to help them with the key words that their information sheet should contain. They could also use some of the printed out photographs from the Resource Gallery to illustrate their sheet.

▶ Look closely with the children at a Newton meter and ask them to explain how it works.

▶ Bring a collection of objects into the classroom. Ask the children to find out the weight of the objects using a Newton meter and to record what the weight is. Reiterate with them that weight is how we measure the downward force of gravity.

▶ Make a collection of relatively heavy objects, such as a brick, a roof tile, a bag of marbles, a large book. Ask the children to predict which one will take the most force to move it and to devise a fair test to find out. (They should use a Newton meter and remember to measure after the object is moving and the initial inertia has been overcome.)

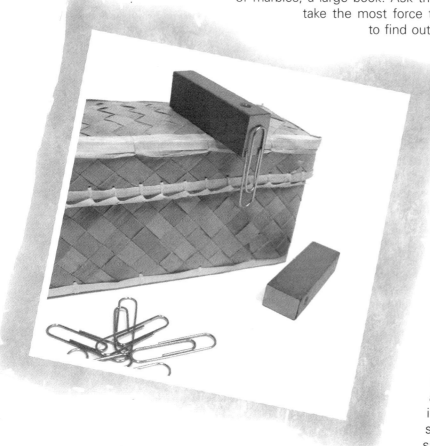

▶ Give the children a copy of the 'Forces in pairs' sheet (photocopiable page 54) and ask them to complete it, labelling each picture with the correct pair of forces at work.

▶ Print out the photographs from the Resource Gallery and give a set to each of the children. Ask them to show the direction of the forces on the photographs by drawing arrows and to label the arrows with the name of the force. For example, the 'Paperclip on bar magnet' would have a downwards pointing arrow labelled *Gravity* and an upwards pointing arrow labelled *Magnetic force*. The children could also label the pictures they drew in their completed 'Forces in pairs' sheet, from the activity above, in the same way.

▶ Make a collection of several different types of paper. Ask the class to devise a fair test to find out how much force is needed to tear each one. Get the children to first predict which paper they think will be the strongest. A good way to organise the test is to wrap each end of the paper round a short length of dowel and fix firmly with sticky tape. Put a large bulldog clip on each piece of dowel. Hang one bulldog clip from a support and attach weights to the other until the paper tears. For safety, make sure that there is a cardboard box under the paper so that the weights can drop into it and not onto children. Ask the children to record the results of the investigation. Were they correct in their prediction of which would be the strongest paper? Finish by asking the children to draw a diagram of the experiment with arrows to show in which direction the forces were acting. They should also label the diagram with the names of the forces involved.

▶ As a class, find out how much force is needed to compress a range of different springs. Put the springs one at a time into a clear, narrow plastic cylinder, such as a measuring cylinder, and balance weights on them until they compress a given distance. Does the heaviest spring need the most force to compress it?

▶ Show the children the effects of air resistance. Use a fluffy feather, a tennis ball and a sheet of typing paper. Ask the children to predict which object will reach the ground first if they are all dropped together. Why do they think this? Devise a fair test to find out and carry out the experiment. Ask the children to write what happened and which forces are acting. (All objects fall at the same speed unless other forces, such as air resistance, are acting.) The feather and the sheet of paper have a larger surface area on which air resistance can act to slow the fall.

▶ Suspend a weight from an elastic band. Ask the children to observe what happens as equal weights are added. Carry out the investigation over a box for the weights to drop safely into should the band snap and, for safety, the children should wear goggles. Can the children predict what will happen to the elastic band as each weight is added? Ask them to watch to see if the elastic band stretches the same amount each time. Is there a pattern in the results? Get them to make a graph.

▶ Make a collection of liquids of different thicknesses (viscosities), such as water, cooking oil, honey or golden syrup. As a class, devise a test to find out if the thickness of a liquid (viscosity) increases the resistance (friction) and affects the rate at which a ball bearing is pulled down (falls) through it. Make sure that the test is fair.

▶ In groups, get the children to experience the upthrust (upwards push) of water and to measure it. Get each group to hang a suitable object, such as a small plastic bag of marbles, from a Newton meter and make a note of how much it weighs. Next, they should weigh the parcel suspended in water. What does it weigh now? Can they write an explanation of the difference in weight?

▶ Show the children how to make parachutes to drop from a height and watch as they are pulled down by gravity. Ask the children to note any other forces that are acting as the parachute falls. For example, air resistance against the underside of the parachute. A parachute is designed to utilise air resistance in order to slow down the fall of the parachutist and this is an example of more than one force acting on an object.

▶ Get the children to draw pictures of parachutists and to label them with the names of the forces acting, including directional arrows.

▶ Look at the photograph 'Astronaut on Moon' again and ask the children to write a poem about what it might be like to walk on the Moon.

▶ In groups, let the children search the Internet to find out more about the expeditions to the Moon that have taken place. Assign a decade to each group to research and then ask the groups to present their findings to the rest of the class.

▶ In groups, get the children to design a Moon colony and to write about what would be needed to sustain it. For example, an artificial atmosphere, a water supply, and so on.

NOTES ON THE PHOTOCOPIABLE PAGES

Word cards

PAGE 53

These word cards contain some of the basic vocabulary for the children to use and learn when learning about 'Forces in action'.

Ask the children to read the words on the cards. Ask which words the children have heard before and review any words they don't understand.

Activities

▶ Read the words to the children and ask them to write down a definition as you do so.
▶ Read some definitions of the words and ask the children to say or write the word to which the definition refers.

Forces in pairs

PAGE 54

This is a sheet to help children identify forces acting and to realise that forces usually act in pairs. Before they start the sheet ask the children to name as many different forces as they can. Make sure they understand that forces usually act in pairs and look again at some of the photographs on the 'Forces in Action' Resource Gallery for the children to name pairs of forces acting.

The forces acting on each of the pictures the children are asked to draw are as follows:

▶ Boat on the ocean: gravity and upthrust
▶ Parachutist: gravity and air resistance (friction)
▶ Magnet holding a nail: gravity and magnetic force
▶ Tug of war: pull and pull
▶ Coconut floating on the sea: gravity and upthrust
▶ Weight lifter holding up a bar with weights on it: gravity and push
▶ Ball falling: gravity and air resistance (friction)
▶ Child tobogganing down a steep slope: gravity and friction
▶ Brick balanced on a spring: gravity and push
▶ Bag of sugar on kitchen scales: gravity and push

Forces word cards

weight

gravity

Newton

force meter

upthrust

Forces in pairs

▶ Draw a picture from the list below in each box.

▶ Label each picture with the correct pair of forces acting on it. The first one has been done for you.

Child sitting on a stool / Parachutist / Magnet holding a nail
Tug of war / Coconut floating on the sea
Weightlifter holding up a bar with weights on it
Ball falling / Child tobogganing down a steep slope
Brick balanced on a spring / Bag of sugar on kitchen scales

Example				
Gravity pulling child down				
Upward force from stool supporting child				

READY RESOURCES ▶▶ S C I E N C E

◣ SCHOLASTIC
PHOTOCOPIABLE

HOW WE SEE THINGS

Content and skills
This chapter links to unit 6F, 'How we see things', of the QCA Scheme of Work for science at Key Stage 2. The 'How We See Things' Resource Gallery on the CD-ROM, together with the teacher's notes and photocopiable pages in this chapter, can be used when teaching this unit.

As with the QCA Scheme of Work, this chapter helps children to understand that we see things when light from a light source, or light reflected from an object, enters our eyes. They learn that light travels from a source and that shadows are formed when the light is blocked in some way. They also learn the difference between shadows and reflections and that the direction in which light travels can be changed by shiny surfaces.

The teacher's notes include ways of using the resources as a whole class, for group work or with individual children. Some of the activities suggested will link with other areas of the curriculum such as English, geography or art. Wherever possible the activities encourage the children to ask questions and develop an enquiring approach to their learning.

Resources on the CD-ROM
The CD-ROM includes photographs showing how mirrors can be used to see awkward places. For example a mirror showing how we see the back of our heads and how the dentist sees all sides of our teeth. A photograph of a side view mirror on a car show how mirrors can be used to improve safety. A photograph of a Hall of Mirrors at a funfair illustrates how mirrors can be used for decorative purposes and how the shape of the mirror affects the image we see.

A photograph of someone reflected in a mirror, and a photograph of the shadow of another person thrown onto a wall, helps to illustrate the difference between a shadow and a reflection for the children.

Photocopiable pages
The photocopiable pages in the book are also provided in PDF format on the CD-ROM and can be printed out from there. They include:
▶ word cards containing the essential vocabulary of the unit
▶ a story retold from Greek mythology
▶ templates to make Indonesian shadow puppets.

Science skills
When using the resources on the CD-ROM and the activities suggested in the teacher's notes, the children will draw upon a wide variety of skills. These include, observing, questioning, finding out, describing, listening, speaking, reading, writing and drawing. For example, explaining the difference between a photograph of a shadow and that of a reflection will help their speaking and listening skills, while finding out which type of surface gives the best reflection will encourage investigative skills.

NOTES ON THE CD-ROM RESOURCES

MIRRORS

Mirror showing back of head, Side mirror on car, Hall of Mirrors at funfair, Dentist's mirror

All objects reflect light, but some reflect more than others. The light enters our eyes enabling us to see things. Mirrors, or other shiny surfaces, reflect light in a particular way enabling us to see images in them.

Mirrors can be used to reflect images from places where it is difficult to see, as the photographs 'Side mirror on car' and the 'Dentist's mirror' show. Two mirrors are used in the photograph where the woman is looking at the back of her head, showing that an image can be reflected from one mirror to another. Mirrors are also used decoratively and for fun, as shown in the photograph 'Hall of Mirrors at funfair'. In this case the mirrors are curved in and out so that the reflected light gives a distorted image.

Make sure that the children understand that we see things because light enters our eyes and not because light is given out from our eyes.

Discussing the photographs

▶ Talk with the children about how we actually see things. Explain that light from a source is reflected by an object and enters our eyes so that we see the object.

▶ Explain that light travels. Remind the children how shadows are formed if the light is blocked. Tell them that a mirror or shiny surface can reflect or change the direction of light.

▶ Look at the photographs with the children and discuss the different ways in which people use mirrors. Talk about how mirrors can be used to see in awkward places. For example in the photograph 'Dentist's mirror' so that the dentist can see behind the teeth or at the very back of the mouth where it's hard to see. The photograph 'Mirror showing back of head' enables the woman to see the back of her head by using two mirrors. Ask the children if they do this, or if a hairdresser has shown them the back of their heads when they have had a hair cut. The photograph 'Side mirror on car' shows children how the driver can see what is happening behind and to the side of the vehicle, thus contributing to road safety.

▶ Can the children think of any other ways that mirrors are used by people to see in awkward places? For example, the mirror on a trolley that can run under a vehicle to check for people trying to smuggle goods in and out of the country, or the mirror on a periscope which enables sailors in submarines to see what is happening on the surface of the water.

▶ Talk about the fact that mirrors are usually made from glass that has a silver film behind it, but that any shiny material will act as a mirror although the image may not be so clear. Can the children think of any shiny surfaces that they sometimes see their reflection in? For example, spoons, shop windows and still water.

▶ Show the children the photograph 'Hall of Mirrors at funfair' and discuss how the shape of a mirror can distort the image we see. Explain how light travels in straight lines and is reflected from a mirror at a similar angle at which it hits it.Therefore, the curves in the mirror in the photograph give a distorted image.

Activities
▶ Ask the children to think about how many mirrors they have at home and what they use them for. Make a list on the board (don't forget the budgie's mirror!).

▶ Ask the children to draw a simple diagram of how they think we see things. This could be done at the start of the unit to find out what children already know and again at the end to assess what they have learned.

▶ Ask the children to write a short piece on how they see things and how images are reflected by mirrors. Give them copies of the 'Reflection word cards' on photocopiable page 60 to help them if appropriate.

▶ As a class, make a list of all the places where mirrors might be found and what they might be used for. For example, in the bathroom for shaving, in the bedroom for putting on make-up or checking clothing, in a shop for trying on new clothes, in a room for decoration or to make it seem larger.

▶ Bring in a torch with a strong, narrow beam. Lie it on some white paper and shine it at a mirror. Ask the children to observe what happens to the beam of light. Move the torch so that it shines on the mirror at a different angle. They should see that the angle of the reflected beam changes.

▶ Use a mirror or several mirrors to redirect a beam of light round the room. A fairly dark room is best for this activity. Ask the children to draw diagrams to explain how the direction of the light was been changed.

▶ If possible find several long pieces of silvered plastic for groups of children to use as a mirror. Let the groups experiment by bending it in different directions to create different images.

▶ Tell the children that mirrors have been used for centuries, but were not always made from glass. Ask them to use the Internet to find out about the things people used to use as mirrors.

▶ Ask the children to try mirror writing. Show them how to write a short message that can only be read by looking at it in a mirror.

▶ Read the story 'Medusa the Gorgon' (photocopiable pages 62–63) taken from Greek mythology and let the children learn how Perseus used his polished shield as a mirror in his quest to slay the Gorgon.

SHADOW OR REFLECTION?

Woman reflected in mirror, Shadow on wall

Help the children to understand the difference between a shadow and a reflection. They need to understand that a shadow is formed when a beam of light is blocked by an object. A reflection is the image we see in a mirror or other shiny surface. All surfaces reflect light, but shiny surfaces are better than dull ones. Light from a source (the Sun) hits an object (a face) which reflects some of it, which in turn hits a shiny object (a mirror). The shiny surface reflects most of the light back so that we appear to see the face in the mirror.

These photographs can be used to aid discussion with the children on reflection and shadows. They both involve people and the children will be able to discuss how the people involved in the photographs are blocking or reflecting light to get different results (a shadow or a reflection).

Discussing the photographs
▶ Ask the children if they can tell you the difference between the two pictures.

▶ Look at the photograph 'Woman reflected in mirror'. Discuss what is happening to the light to create the reflection in the mirror.

▶ Look at the photograph 'Shadow on wall' and discuss how the shadow has been created in scientific terms.

▶ Look again and discuss the amount of detail that can be seen in each picture. Which is the clearer? Why? Can you see details of the features in the shadow? Why not?

▶ Discuss why shadows usually appear black, while reflections are in full colour. Explain to the children that when a shadow is cast the light is blocked and not reflected back into the eye. With a mirror almost all the light is reflected and, therefore, we see the object in colour.

Activities
▶ Make a collection of objects with shiny and dull surfaces. Ask the children to consider which act as the best mirrors. What generalisation do the children think can be made about

these surfaces? Are the shiny surfaces or the dull ones the best reflectors?

▶ Ask the children to choose a surface that reflects and to make a self-portrait copying the image they see. Let them experiment with different surfaces and choose an appropriate medium for their portrait. For example pastel might be a good medium to use if the reflection is rather indistinct and fuzzy.

▶ Divide the class into groups. Pin sheets of black paper at various points around the classroom, creating an area of black paper for each group. Show the children how to use a bright light to throw shadows onto the sheets of paper. Show them how to draw round the shadow with chalk and cut it out to make a silhouette. The children can make silhouettes of all the people in their group for others to recognise. Is a silhouette easier to recognise if it is made from someone's profile or their face front-on?

▶ Ask the children to write a short explanation of the difference between shadow formation and reflection in terms of the path of a light beam. Give them copies of the 'Shadows word cards' on photocopiable page 61 to prompt them with key words if appropriate. They could also draw a diagram to accompany their description.

▶ Give the children copies of the 'Indonesian shadow puppets' (photocopiable pages 64–67). Let them make the puppets and, in groups, put on their own shadow puppet performance.

NOTES ON THE PHOTOCOPIABLE PAGES

Word cards 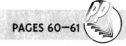 PAGES 60–61

These word cards contain some of the basic vocabulary for the children to use and learn when looking at 'How we see things'. These include:

▶ words associated with reflection
▶ words associated with shadows.

Ask the children to read through the words and ask for clarification if there any new or unfamiliar ones.

Activities

▶ Use the words *reflection* and *shadow* from the word cards to illustrate their meaning. Hold the *shadow* card in a beam of light to form a shadow. Hold the *reflection* card in front of a mirror so that the word can be seen as a reflection. Discuss with the children why it is difficult to read.

▶ Use the word cards as a word bank to help the children label pictures or to help them with their writing. Add new words that are appropriate to your class as you teach the unit.

▶ Ask the children to find out which letters of the alphabet look the same when reflected in a mirror as they do without. Demonstrate how to do so by holding a mirror at right angles in front of some text. Can they make any words using these letters? (For example, HIDE.)

▶ Ask the children to find some words that make different words when reflected in a mirror. For example, *pop* reads *bob*.

Medusa the Gorgon  PAGES 62–63

This is a story taken from Greek mythology. It tells how Perseus used his shield as a mirror to enable him to kill Medusa without having to look directly at the Gorgon's hideous head, which would have been a fatal move. The story ties in well with the work the children will have done on light reflecting off shiny surfaces.

Discussing the text

▶ Read the story to the children. Ask them what Perseus's shield was made of. Get them to explain to you how it reflected the image of Medusa if it did not have a mirror as a front. Talk about how shiny surfaces can act as mirrors, as Perseus's shield did.

▶ Talk about the surfaces that would have been used as mirrors before glass was discovered. For example, the still surface of water, shiny stones or metal.

Activities

▶ Let the children experiment with various objects that have different surfaces to find out which makes the best mirror.

▶ Ask the children to find out about other stories that involve mirrors. For example, Alice's adventures in *Through the Looking Glass*, and *Snow White and the Seven Dwarfs*.

▶ Let the children try writing secret messages in mirror writing for others to decode.

▶ Help the children make a small piece of Indian mirror work embroidery. They could turn this into a purse or bookmark.

Indonesian shadow puppets   PAGES 64–67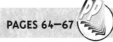

Shadow puppets are great fun for children, and cultures such as that of Indonesia have developed them into an art form. These outlines can be cut out and made into puppets by the children by adding sticks to them making joints by inserting paper fasteners at the shoulder, elbow, hip and knee.

This sheet works well to reinforce children's learning about how shadows are formed by blocking the light.

Discussing the shadow puppets

▶ Indonesian shadow puppets are an old art form and are used to tell traditional stories. Talk about how the puppets are moved using sticks attached to the arms and legs of the model.

▶ Discuss with the children how the shadow puppet theatre works. Explain that bright light is shone behind a screen and the puppets placed between the light and the screen, thus blocking the light and creating a shadow.

▶ Talk about the complexity of some of the figures used in Indonesian shadow puppet theatres that may be many years old. Explain how their limbs are jointed to allow them to move more realistically and how they are often beautifully decorated, even though the decorations don't really show up in the shadows they make.

Activities

▶ Let the children make the shadow puppets. They could decorate their puppets and perforate them in places, to let some light through to make them more interesting. For example, they could cut out the eyes to give the impression that they are shining.

▶ In groups, show the children how to make a simple shadow theatre from a sheet of opaque paper with a good light source behind it. Ask the children to experiment to find the optimum distance from the screen to give the clearest shadow. They could also experiment using different distances from the screen to layer and give depth to the scene.

▶ Let groups of children write a short play to perform to the rest of the class.

▶ Encourage the children to use the Internet or other sources to find out more about Indonesian shadow puppet theatres.

▶ Ask the children to find Indonesia on an atlas.

reflect

reflection

light beam

mirror

light travelling

image

Shadows word cards

shadow
silhouette
blocked light
opaque
transparent
translucent
distance
clarity

Medusa the Gorgon (1)

Perseus was a great Greek hero of mythology and son of the god Zeus. When he grew to be a man, Polydectes, his mother's suitor, gave him a seemingly impossible task (Polydectes secretly wanted Perseus dead). The task given him was to slay the monster Medusa, one of the three Gorgon sisters.

Medusa's very looks were deadly, even to the best armed enemy. To punish her for an unkindly act the goddess Athene had turned Medusa's hair into deadly vipers that writhed about her face. So dreadful and horrible were her looks that whoever looked on her face was instantly transfixed and turned to stone before he could strike even one blow.

Perseus was not afraid of the monster and made himself ready for mortal combat. Athene the goddess gave him wise counsel."Without the help of the gods, not even the bravest of men could kill such a foe," she said.

Athene and her brother, the god Hermes, lent Perseus some powerful and magical aids to help him in his task. Hermes gave him his own crooked sword that could cut through any armour. He fitted the young man's feet with winged sandals to take him swiftly over both land and sea. He also gave him a wonderful helmet that made the wearer invisible. Athene gave him her shield. It was a shield so highly polished that it reflected any scene before it like a mirror. Athene warned Perseus that on no account must he look on the Gorgon's face. If he did, he would be turned to stone. Athene told him he must use the shield like a mirror and look at Medusa's reflection so that he might strike off her head and kill her without ever looking at her face. She also gave Perseus a goatskin bag to carry the head away in, because even in death it would freeze the blood of any who looked at it.

Thus, properly equipped, Perseus set off to find the faraway isle where Medusa had her lair. Springing off the cliffs of Seriphos he flew north, as he had been told to do, to find the three old Graiae sisters, for only they could tell him the way to Medusa's lair. He travelled to lands of snow and ice so cold that no mortal man could live there. He found the three sisters huddled up together, dim and shapeless. They were so old that they only had one eye and one tooth between them. These they passed and fumbled from one to the other as they needed, to munch the snowflakes or to peer through the icy and blinding mists.

READY RESOURCES ▶▶ S C I E N C E

📣 SCHOLASTIC
PHOTOCOPIABLE

Medusa the Gorgon (2)

As Athene had told him to, Perseus crept up on the sisters and stole their single eye.

"Tell me the way to the Gorgons," he demanded, "or I'll steal your tooth also and leave you to perish in this miserable wilderness." The sisters wailed and cried and demanded that he give them back their eye, but when they saw that he held firm they mumbled the way to the Gorgons' lair.

Then off Perseus flew to the hottest lands in the world, where the earth lay green with fields and trees, and the sky and sea were the bluest of blues. There he found the island where the hateful Gorgon sisters lived and saw them asleep in the midday sun, Medusa in the middle. He did not dare look with his eyes but, as Athene had instructed him, he came near with his back turned holding up the shield to make a mirror for that blood-curdling head. Its mane of viper hair was writhing and moving about it even as Medusa slept. The shield mirror trembled in his hand as Perseus saw that the Gorgon's face was fearfully beautiful as well as horrible. Then, in the mirror, Perseus saw that her body was covered with loathsome scales and bronze-coloured feathers, and that her four limbs ended in dreadful claws. Her open mouth was full of fangs bristling round her forked tongue. Her lips were parted in a bitter smile. Fascinated as he was, he dared not look any longer for fear that she should wake and open her terrible eyes.

Noting in his mirror how and where she lay, he drew his sword and struck backwards with all his strength, severing the hideous head with one blow. As the sword cut clean through her neck she uttered one small cry. Still using the mirror to guide him, Perseus picked up the horrific head, upon which the vipers were trembling and moving, even in death, and shoved it into the goatskin bag. He tied the mouth of the bag tightly with a piece of strong leather brought for the purpose.

Medusa's small death cry had woken her sisters who, seeing their sister dead, spread their wings and like monstrous birds of prey, tried to attack him. Perseus hid from them by putting on the helmet of invisibility and flew off carrying the sack. As he flew the Gorgon's blood dripped through the sack onto the earth and turned into venomous scorpions and snakes that have plagued the world ever since.

Retold by Gay Wilson

Indonesian shadow puppet (1)

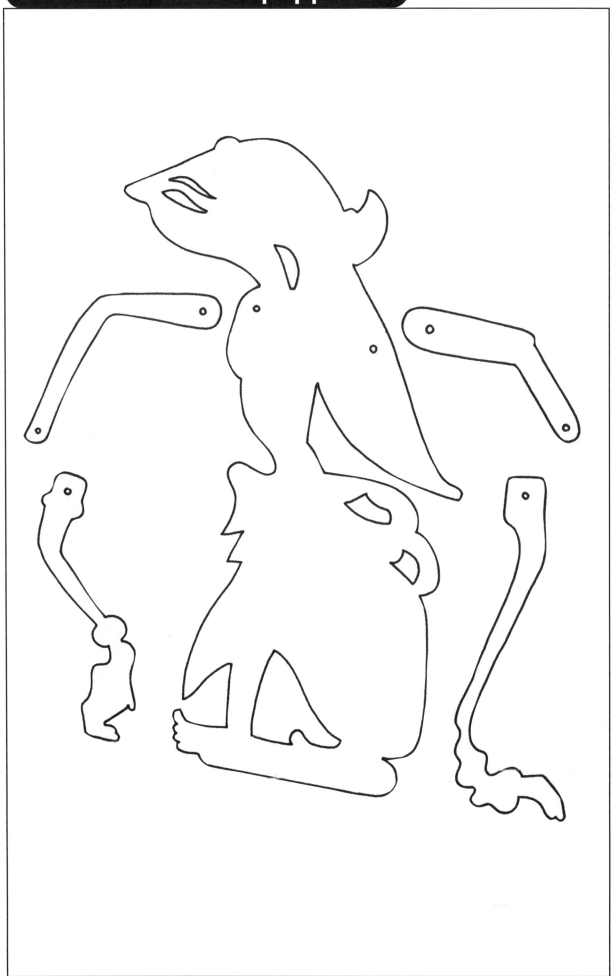

📖 SCHOLASTIC
PHOTOCOPIABLE

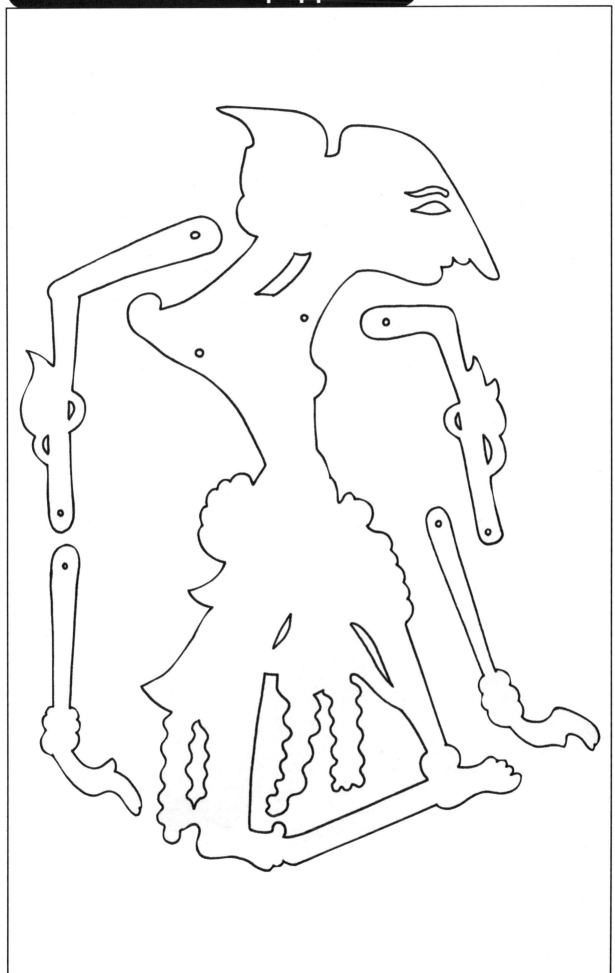

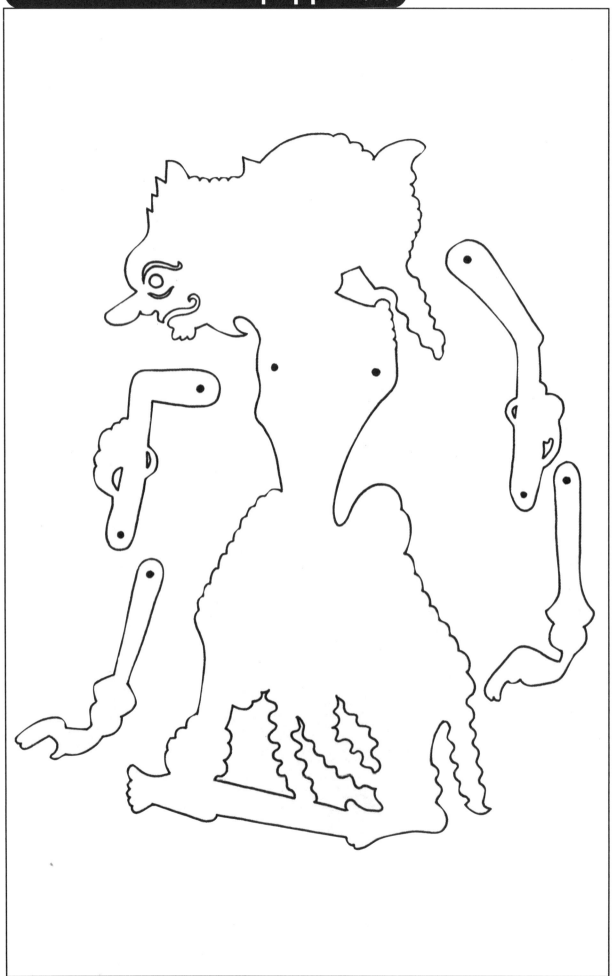

Indonesian shadow puppet (4)

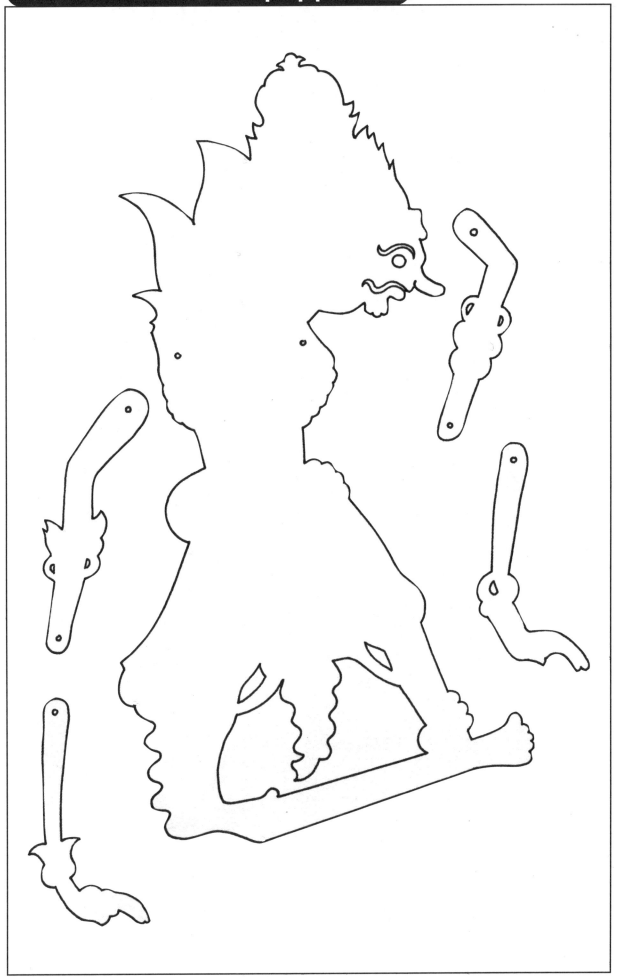

CHANGING CIRCUITS

Content and skills

This chapter links to Unit 6G, 'Changing circuits', of the QCA Scheme of Work for science at Key Stage 2. The Changing Circuits Resource Gallery on the CD-ROM, together with the teacher's notes and photocopiable pages in this chapter, can be used when teaching this unit.

As with the QCA Scheme of Work, this chapter helps children to revise the work on electricity that they did in Year 2 and Year 4. They revisit work on conductors and insulators, and work on being safe around electricity. They also learn the value of using standard symbols to represent components in a circuit so that other people can understand their plans and diagrams.

The teacher's notes in this chapter include ways of using the resources as a whole class, for group work or with individual children. Some of the activities suggested will link with other areas of the curriculum such as English, maths, history and art. Wherever possible the activities encourage the children to ask questions and develop an enquiring approach to their learning.

Resources on the CD-ROM

The CD-ROM contains a number of photographs to support the children's learning for this unit. Illustrations of road safety signs introduce the children to the importance of symbols. This can be built on by using the illustrations of electrical component symbols so that the children understand that these are universal and why they are used. A more complicated circuit diagram from an alternating flasher is included so that the children understand that all electrical appliances have a complete circuit and that some have many. Photographs of a fuse box and an overloaded electrical socket can be used to teach the importance of being safe around electricity.

Photocopiable pages

The photocopiable pages in the book are also provided in PDF format on the CD-ROM and can be printed out from there. They include:
▶ word cards containing the essential vocabulary of the unit
▶ a biography of Michael Faraday
▶ a text sheet on the National grid
▶ a test sheet about being safe around electricity.

Science skills

Skills such as observing, questioning, finding out, describing, sorting, sequencing, listening, speaking, reading, writing and drawing are involved in the activities suggested for the unit in the teacher's notes. For example, observing road signs, discussing why they are different shapes and how they help to keep us safe will develop the children's speaking and listening skills. Information sheets on Michael Faraday and the National grid will encourage reading and comprehension skills. Finding out and researching skills are encouraged in many activities, by encouraging the children to gain information about famous scientists from the Internet or by using other secondary sources.

NOTES ON THE CD-ROM RESOURCES

SYMBOLS

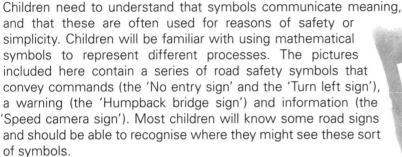

No entry sign, Turn left sign, Humpback bridge sign, Speed camera sign, Electrical component symbols

Children need to understand that symbols communicate meaning, and that these are often used for reasons of safety or simplicity. Children will be familiar with using mathematical symbols to represent different processes. The pictures included here contain a series of road safety symbols that convey commands (the 'No entry sign' and the 'Turn left sign'), a warning (the 'Humpback bridge sign') and information (the 'Speed camera sign'). Most children will know some road signs and should be able to recognise where they might see these sort of symbols.

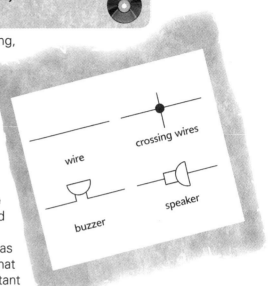

Children need to understand how electrical symbols contribute to clarifying circuit diagrams and help in their construction and maintenance.

The children also need to know that some symbols, such as electrical component symbols, are used internationally so that people of all nationalities can understand them. This is important since electrical goods are made in different countries and exported all over the world.

Discussing the pictures

▶ Talk with the children about why symbols are used in many everyday contexts. Talk about how one symbol can represent lots of words and is quicker to draw than a picture.
▶ Discuss the fact that many symbols are international and can be understood by people who speak different languages.
▶ Look at the four pictures of road safety symbols and discuss what each one represents with the children. Explain how it is important for drivers and pedestrians to understand signs on the roads immediately, and that a symbol can give this information very quickly.
▶ Talk about the different shapes of the signs and how this gives more information. For example, the round signs with a red circle around them, such as the 'No entry sign' and the 'Turn left sign', give orders and must be obeyed. Triangular signs, such as the 'Humpback bridge sign', give warnings of hazards ahead. Rectangular signs, such as the 'Speed camera sign', give information (ie telling drivers there are cameras to enforce speed regulations).
▶ Discuss how understanding what road signs mean helps to keep people safe on the roads.
▶ Look at the illustration 'Electrical component symbols' and ask the children to tell you what each represents. Talk about why it is important for people working with electricity to understand these symbols. Discuss how this can help to keep them safe.
▶ Ask the children if they can think of other areas where symbols are used. For example, mathematics, hazard warning labels, plant labels, weather symbols, and so on.

Activities

▶ Ask the children to make a series of simple circuits and then represent them as circuit diagrams, using symbols, for others to construct.
▶ Give the children the 'Simple circuits' sheet (photocopiable page 77) to construct circuits from. They can also use the 'Electrical component symbols' to help them substitute the drawings on the sheet.
▶ Ask the children to find out about other road signs. Are other shapes used for signs other than those they've already looked at? Ask them to find signs that they think might be appropriate for the area around their school.
▶ Ask the children to make a list of all the road signs passed on the way to school, or in the immediate vicinity. Get them to sort these into orders, warnings, information, and so on.
▶ Challenge the children to create a set of symbols to represent the school rules. For example, a running figure with a cross through it to represent 'no running in the corridors'.

CIRCUIT DIAGRAMS

Circuit diagram: Alternating flasher

Children need to understand that all types of electrical equipment need complete circuits in order for them to work. A piece of equipment will often have more than one circuit and it is important that there is a 'map' of these circuits so that the equipment may be efficiently and safely maintained. To this end most service handbooks that accompany electrical goods contain a circuit diagram.

Discussing the illustration
▶ Ask the children to tell you what they remember about simple circuits. Remind them that a complete circuit is needed in order to make a device work.
▶ Look at the illustration 'Circuit diagram: Alternating flasher' and ask how it differs from the simple circuits they have seen before. Talk about how it is more complicated, but that there must still be a complete circuit, or circuits, if the device is to work.
▶ Discuss the symbols used in the diagram. Do they recognise any of them? What does each one represent? Why are symbols used instead of little pictures?
▶ Look at the diagram again. Is there more than one circuit?
▶ Explain what electrical device this circuit diagram comes from. Talk about why electrical devices have circuit diagrams like this one. Explain how the circuit diagram helps the maintenance engineers to trace faults if a machine breaks down.

Activities
▶ Give each child a copy of the 'Circuit diagram: Alternating flasher' and ask them to trace the path of one complete circuit within it. They should highlight the components using a coloured pen or pencil and then make a list of them.
▶ Challenge the children to draw a circuit diagram for wiring a robot that has two eyes that light up, a nose that flashes and a buzzer for a voice.
▶ Get the children to make each other's circuits from the above activity to ensure they work.

FUSED/OVERLOADED

Fuse box, Overloaded electrical socket

Fuses are designed to fail or burn out and break the circuit if it is overloaded or a fault occurs. This helps prevent damage to the equipment or the possibility of fire. Fuses are made of resistance wire.

Nichrome wire is a readily available resistance wire for use in the classroom. It enables children to experience putting resistance into a circuit to make a bulb burn less brightly or a motor turn more slowly. Modern fuses often consist of a short length of resistance or fuse wire in a small capsule, such as those in three pin electric plugs.

Children need to understand that electricity can be dangerous. Overloaded circuits can create heat which could be sufficient to cause a fire. These days a home may have far more electrical devices than it has socket outlets and there is a temptation to overload a socket by using various adapters, as in the photograph 'Overloaded electrical socket'. Children should learn that this is a dangerous practice.

Discussing the photographs
▶ Look at the photograph 'Fuse box' with the children and discuss the fact that a fuse is there to protect a circuit and prevent equipment being damaged.
▶ Talk about the difference between ordinary insulated wire and resistance (fuse) wire. Discuss the thinness of the wire and how it is meant to burn out if too much current is passed through it.
▶ Explain to the children that there are different thicknesses of fuse wire according to how much current the circuit is expected to carry. A washing machine with a heater in it would use a thicker wire than a table lamp.
▶ Talk about the fact that some modern circuits may have a different type of fuse that breaks the circuit without burning through. These can be often be reset by pressing a switch.
▶ Discuss the dangers of overloading a circuit. Look at 'Overloaded electrical socket' and

talk about how this could cause the socket to overheat and could possibly start a fire.
▶ Talk about why sockets are sometimes overloaded. Ask the children to suggest safer answers to the problem of more plugs than sockets, as shown in the photograph.

Activities
▶ Show the children a modern fuse capsule. Talk about the number on it, for example 13A, indicating the amount of current it is designed to carry.
▶ Demonstrate to the children the result of overloading and burning out (blowing) a fuse. Use one strand of wire wool and, using tongs or a wooden clothes peg, hold it between the terminals of a 6v battery. The wire will glow and burn through. (Make sure you observe all the appropriate safety precautions.)
▶ Ask the children to look around the school or at home for overloaded sockets. Get them to write a report and suggest alternative strategies, such as extension leads or the repositioning of equipment to use empty sockets.
▶ Many classrooms are inadequately supplied with electrical sockets. Draw a plan of the classroom on the board and encourage the children to suggest where sockets could be usefully fitted to ensure that there are no trailing wires or overloaded sockets. Indicate the children's suggestions on the plan.
▶ Bring a collection of fuses in and ask the children to find out what equipment each would be used for. They could look at labels on electrical appliances or in instruction manuals and match them to the correct fuse.
▶ Let the children use resistance wire to vary the current in a circuit. Challenge them to investigate how to make a bulb dimmer or how to alter the speed of an electric motor.

COMPLETE CIRCUITS

Engineer working on computer server

Make sure that the children understand that electrical circuits can be very complicated and should never be tampered with in any way. The mains supply should always be switched off before, for example, pulling a plug from a socket, changing a fuse, and so on.

Discussing the photograph
▶ Look at the photograph with the class and discuss what is happening. Talk about how people need to be properly trained to work with electricity.
▶ Look at the wires in the photograph and ask the children to note how they are different colours. Particularly in complex set-ups, it important engineers can differentiate the wires they are working with. Talk about how wires are usually covered by an insulating material to prevent the bare wires touching each other and causing a short circuit.
▶ Talk about how the different coloured insulation covering helps to identify which wire is which. Talk about metal being a good conductor of electricity, while plastic and rubber are very poor conductors and, therefore, make good insulators. Explain that other materials, such as water, will also conduct electricity.
▶ Talk about how insulation is important in preventing electric shocks.

Activities
▶ Show the children a piece of covered wire. Use wire strippers to remove part of the insulation and to show them how the wire is covered. Ask the children to draw a picture of it and to label the conductor and the insulator. Give them copies of 'Circuits word cards (1)' on photocopiable page 74 to help them with the labelling if appropriate.
▶ Get the children to write a definition of an insulator and a conductor.
▶ Give the children a copy of the 'Michael Faraday' biography (photocopiable page 78) to find out about Michael Faraday and his discoveries.
▶ Ask the children to find out more about other people in history who worked with electricity, such as Humphry Davy.
▶ Suggest the children imagine a world without electricity and write an account of what it would be like.
▶ Give the children a copy of the 'National grid' sheet (photocopiable page 79) and read it through with them. Use it to stress the dangers of electricity, and that they shouldn't go near electricity sources such as those described in the text.

NOTES ON THE PHOTOCOPIABLE PAGES

Word cards
PAGES 74–76

These word cards contain some of the basic vocabulary for the children to use and learn when looking at 'Changing circuits'. These include:
▶ words associated with circuits
▶ words associated with electricity distribution.
Ask the children to read through the words on the sheets and define any words which are new or unfamiliar.

Activities
▶ Cut the word cards out and laminate them. Use them as often as possible with the children when teaching this unit.
▶ Use the word cards in displays of work on this unit.
▶ Use the word cards as a word bank to help the children label pictures or to help them with their writing.

Simple circuits
PAGE 77

This is a sheet of simple circuits using symbols of the component parts for the children to label and then to make each circuit.

Discussing the circuits
▶ Ask the children to tell you why we use internationally agreed symbols for the components in electrical circuits. (Because they do not rely on language to be understood.)
▶ Tell the children that people buying a television in Sweden need to be able to understand how to install and run an appliance made in Japan. International symbols help people around the world to be able to use electrical equipment made in other countries.

Activities
▶ Ask the children to complete the sheet individually or complete it as a class, talking through the symbols that can be substituted for the drawings.
▶ If appropriate, give the children a copy of the 'Electrical component symbols' from the Changing Circuits Resource Gallery. They can use this as reference for replacing the drawings with the correct symbols.

Michael Faraday
PAGE 78

This is a short biography of Michael Faraday, the man who realised the potential of electrical energy and devoted much of his life to its advancement.

Discussing the text
▶ Read the text with the children and review the main discoveries that Michael Faraday made during his life. Why were these important?
▶ Talk with the children about how scientists often have to carry out many, many experiments before they make a scientific breakthrough. Explain how people like Faraday persevered with their ideas, often against strong opposition at the time.

Activities
▶ Ask the children to find out more about Michael Faraday.
▶ Get the children to write an article about Faraday as if it were to be published in a newspaper of that time.
▶ Challenge the children to find out what Sir Humphry Davy was most famous for.
▶ Make a class book about famous scientists. The children could use the Internet, or other information sources, to find the information they need.

National grid

PAGE 79

It is important that children know that electricity is a major source of energy, but that it has to be generated using a fuel, such as coal, gas, oil and, in some cases, nuclear fuel. A very small amount of our electricity is generated from renewable resources, such as wind, water and solar energy. Electricity is very safe if treated with respect, used properly and the safety rules followed.

Discussing the text

▶ Read the text through with the children and make sure they understand what the National grid is. Ensure that the safety issues are also understood.

▶ Talk about how it would not be practical for each factory or house to have its own generator. Therefore, power stations generate electricity on a large scale and distribute it around the country.

▶ Explain how most power stations use fossil fuels which pollute the atmosphere.

Activities

▶ Use the 'Electricity distribution word cards' on photocopiable page 76 to familiarise the children with the key words in the text.

▶ Ask the children to use books or the Internet to find out about generating electricity using renewable sources, such as water, wind or solar power.

▶ As a class, write to a local electricity company and request information about the source of the electricity that they supply and what fuel is used to generate it.

▶ As a class, map any pylons or sub-stations on a local map.

▶ Ask the children to think about, and make a list of, ways in which we could use less electricity in our everyday lives.

▶ In groups, get the children to design a poster warning of the dangers of playing near pylons or sub-stations.

▶ Ask the children to look around at home and to make a list of all the electrical devices that are working at one time. Are they all necessary? How could they save electricity?

▶ Challenge the children to find out how much it costs to keep one light on for a day, a week and a year.

▶ Give the children a copy of 'How safe are you?' (photocopiable page 80) to assess the children's knowledge of electrical safety.

How safe are you?

PAGE 80

This is a question sheet to test children's knowledge about safety around electricity. It could be used as an individual test sheet or as a basis for discussion, either in groups or with the whole class. It would also be a useful assessment of the children's knowledge at the end of teaching this unit.

Circuit word cards (1)

complete circuits

conductor

insulator

circuit symbol

component

circuit diagram

Circuit word cards (2)

voltage

cell

battery

fuse

fused

sub-stations

power stations

national grid

pylons

cables

Simple circuits

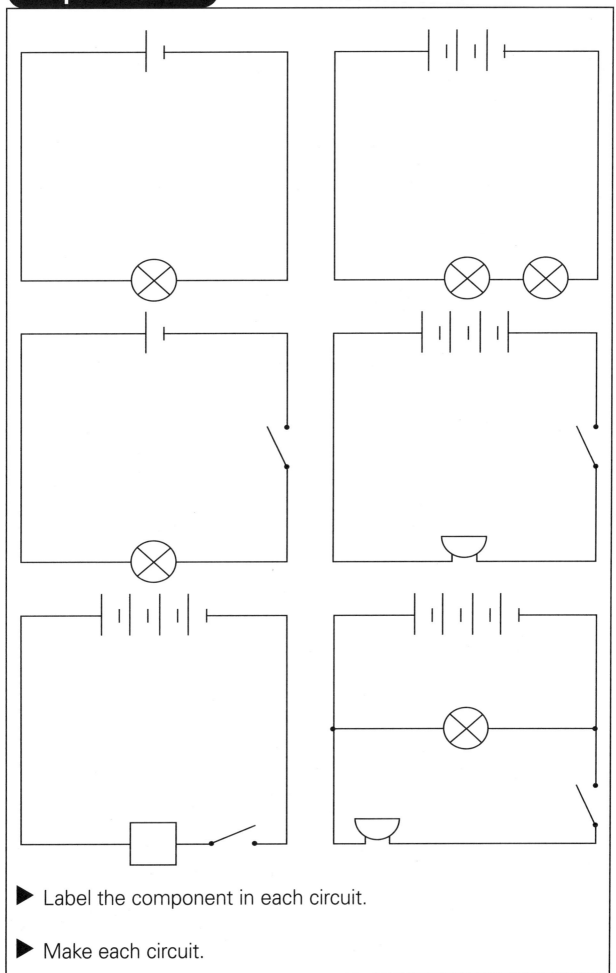

▶ Label the component in each circuit.

▶ Make each circuit.

Michael Faraday (1791–1867)

Michael Faraday was born in London on 22 September 1791. His father was a blacksmith, however in 1805, at the age of 14, Michael was apprenticed to a bookbinder. During his seven year apprenticeship there he developed an interest in science, particularly in chemistry.

In 1810 he joined the City Philosophical Society, where young people met to discuss scientific topics. In 1812, towards the end of his apprenticeship with the bookbinder, he was given a ticket to hear Humphry Davy, a well-known scientist of the day, lecture at the Royal Institution.

Faraday was very impressed with what he heard at the lecture and wrote to Davy later that year, asking for a position working with him in science. Faraday also sent the notes he had made at the lecture with his letter and as a result was appointed Chemical Assistant at the Royal Institution in 1813.

Hans Christian Oersted had discovered electro-magnetism by this time and Faraday became interested in this topic. Through a series of experiments he discovered electro-magnetic rotation, which is the principle behind the electric motor. However, his work on this lapsed for about ten years while he worked on other things. During this time he discovered the chemical benzene and worked on making optical glass.

In 1826 he began giving what became known as his Friday Evening Discourses. Between 1826 and 1862 he gave 123 of these Discourses, and they helped establish his reputation as a great scientist of the day. Also contributing to this reputation were the Christmas Lectures, which he founded and gave, at the Royal Institution. Both the Friday Evening Discourses and the Christmas Lectures still go on today.

Ten years later Faraday returned to his work on electro-magnetism. In 1831 he discovered electro-magnetic induction. This is the principle behind what we know today as the transformer and the generator. It was discoveries such as this that enabled electricity to become a useful and important part of everyday lives, rather than a curiosity.

Faraday continued to work on electricity. For a time he worked with Trinity House trying to develop more efficient lighthouses. He also spent a considerable amount of time trying to develop electric lighting. But all this work took its toll, and he became ill and died at Hampton Court on 25 August 1867. He is buried in Highgate Cemetery, where a lot of famous people are buried.

© SODA

READY RESOURCES ▶▶ S C I E N C E

National grid

Electricity is a source of energy that can be quickly and conveniently converted into heat, light or movement. Most of the electricity we use is generated in large power stations using fossil fuels, such as coal, oil or gas. However, there is concern about the amount of pollution and greenhouse gases given off by this type of power station.

Some power stations use nuclear fuels, but there is also concern about the safety of using nuclear fuels, particularly after disasters like Chernobyl.

In some areas, such as Scotland or Wales, it is possible to use water to turn the huge turbines that generate electricity. These hydroelectric generators are clean and efficient, but are only feasible in mountainous areas. A great deal of research is being carried out into the use of renewable energy sources, such as wind or waves.

Electricity generated in power stations is distributed to homes, factories or offices around the country by a system known as the national grid. This is a network of cables, sometimes buried underground, but often carried overland by huge pylons. This grid is connected so that electricity can be diverted from one area to another to meet demand.

The cables supported by the pylons carry very high voltages – around 30, 000 volts. This high voltage of electricity is converted at local sub-stations to a lower voltage suitable for domestic use. Sub-stations carry electricity to households, businesses or schools. The usual household supply in this country is 240 volts.

Because of the high voltage of electricity in the cables carried by pylons it is extremely dangerous to try climbing them. Similarly, sub-stations are not suitable places to play.

Batteries that people use to power electrical goods can have a supply of 1.5, 4.5, 6 or 9 volts, which is much lower than that carried by cables and sub-stations. Because the mains supply of electricity has much more energy than that in batteries it can be very dangerous if not treated with due respect. It can start fires, produce electric shocks or even kill people because of a short circuit which creates great heat. For example, if bare wires are touched the current will short circuit through the body. Electricity is safe to use in the home as long as it is treated safely.

Answer these questions to find out how safe you are around

How safe are you?

electricity:

1. Why are wires usually covered in plastic?

_____

_____

_____

_____

2. Is it safe to take electrical equipment to bits? Why/why not?

_____

_____

_____

_____

3. Is it sensible to play near or climb pylons? Why/why not?

_____

_____

_____

_____

4. Why shouldn't you fly a kite near overhead cables?

_____

_____

_____

_____

5. Why are electrical sub-stations places to avoid?

_____

_____

_____

_____

6. Why are there usually no electrical sockets, other than shaver points, in a bathroom?

_____

_____

_____

READY RESOURCES ▶▶ S C I E N C E

SCHOLASTIC
PHOTOCOPIABLE